THE EYE O...

David Adam was born ... land, and is now the ... over twenty years he was the Vicar of Danby in North Yorkshire, where he discovered a gift for composing prayers in the Celtic pattern. His first book of these, *The Edge of Glory*, achieved immediate popularity. Most of the material in this book has already been tried and tested with small groups from his own parish and on retreats.

THE EYE
OF THE EAGLE

---

*Meditations on the Hymn
'Be thou my vision'*

DAVID ADAM

*Illustrated by
Peter Dingle and others*

TRIANGLE

First published 1990
Triangle
SPCK
Holy Trinity Church
Marylebone Road
London NW1 4DU

British Library Cataloguing in Publication Data
Adam, David, *1936–*
The eye of the eagle: meditations on the hymn "Be thou my vision"
1. Christian life. Devotional works
I. Title
242

ISBN 0-281-04480-5

Typeset by Rowland Phototypesetting Ltd
Bury St Edmunds, Suffolk
Printed in Great Britain by
BPCC Hazell Books
Aylesbury, Bucks, England
Member of BPCC Ltd

ACKNOWLEDGEMENTS

Once more I am indebted to the artists who have contemplated the mysteries and shared in their wonder. My thanks to Denise Adam, Laura Dingle, Peter Dingle and Jean Freer. Their art is well worth meditating upon.

Many thanks to Will Taylor for his love of the world, and for portraying it through his art. Once more the cover is an expression of the beyond in our midst.

To Denise who enjoys and endures with me the pilgrimage we are on, and has extended my love for this earth.

To the people of Danby, Castleton, and Commondale
for the mysteries we have explored together and the
common vision we have shared.

Contents

___

Be thou my vision, O Lord of my heart,
be all else but naught to me, save that thou art;
be thou my best thought in the day and the night,
both waking and sleeping, thy presence my light.

Be thou my wisdom, be thou my true word,
be thou ever with me, and I with thee, Lord;
be thou my great Father, and I thy true son;
be thou in me dwelling, and I with thee one.

Be thou my breastplate, my sword for the fight;
be thou my whole armour, be thou my true might;
be thou my soul's shelter, be thou my strong tower:
O raise thou me heavenward, great Power of my power.

Riches I heed not, nor man's empty praise;
be thou mine inheritance now and always;
be thou and thou only the first in my heart;
O Sovereign of heaven, my treasure thou art.

High King of heaven, thou heaven's bright Sun,
O grant me its joys after vict'ry is won;
great Heart of my own heart, whatever befall,
still be thou my vision, thou Ruler of all.

8th century Irish
Translated Mary Byrne (1880–1931)
versified Eleanor Hull (1860–1935)

Introduction

The hymn 'Be thou my vision' comes from Ireland and was written somewhere between the eighth and tenth centuries. So it has been sung and used for over a thousand years. The images it uses go back at least a further thousand years to the beginnings of Christianity and before that to the Old Testament. Like much of the Celtic literature, for a good part of this last thousand years it has remained 'lost' to general use. Now that it has been found again, it comes to us with freshness and a challenge like the early morning. It deserves our time and will deeply reward our meditations.

As you would expect with a hymn, the images repeat themselves over and over. This is reflected in the meditations that will return to a theme and seek to build on it. Do not skip over this area and think that you have been there before; remember that there is great depth here – and the treasure is waiting to be found by you and enjoyed. An experience is often like driving home a nail, it cannot be achieved in one blow. To reap benefit from meditation, we have to cover the same ground often and discover new beauties and new wonders.

The images used in this hymn are common to the early Church, yet are expressed here in a particularly Celtic way. The Celtic Church's beginnings are lost in the mists of time. The first Christians to visit Britain and Ireland were probably traders from the Mediterranean. During the lifetime of Jesus trade was well established between the whole of the Mediterranean area and our lands. Because of the Gulf Stream, it is interesting to see that the earliest maps put Ireland closer to the Mediterranean than Britain. It is an interesting thought that the ships that Paul watched at Joppa could well have been setting off for or returning from Ireland. It is of note that in the Eastern Church, by the fifth century, there is a tradition that St Paul, or his disciple Aristobulus, had preached to the Britons. Gildas, Britain's own historian from the sixth century, says, 'Christ the True Son, afforded His light, the knowledge of His precepts, to our island in the last year, as we know, of Tiberius Caesar.' If we could accept this tradition, or the Glastonbury traditions, as correct, then Christianity came to these islands within the first ten years after the Resurrection. There is a further legend that some Judaean Christians were welcomed at the court of King Caractacus. We do not get on very firm ground until AD 314 and the Council of Arles, when the British Church was large enough to send three bishops to attend. However it started, we know that the Celtic Church was in existence well before Saint Augustine, or for that matter Saint Patrick.

I have used the versified translation of the hymn for three reasons. First, I believe that it captures best the original feeling of rhythm and of great themes repeating themselves. Then because it is better known in this form and it is more memorable. This verse form is by Eleanor Hull who lived from 1860 to 1935.

However, I thought you might also like to look at some of the hymn in its more literal translation by Mary Byrne. If nothing else, this will help you to see how closely our hymn keeps to the original:

1   Be thou my vision, beloved Lord: no other is aught but the King of the seven heavens.

2   Be thou my meditation by day and night: may it be thou that I behold for ever in my sleep.

3   Be thou my speech, be thou my understanding: be thou for me; may I be for thee.

4   Be thou my father; may I be thy son: mayest thou be mine; may I be thine.

5   Be thou my battle-shield, be thou my sword: be thou my honour, be thou my delight.

6   Be thou my shelter, be thou my stronghold: mayest thou raise me up in the company of angels.

7   Be thou every good to my body and soul: be thou my kingdom in heaven and earth.

8   Be thou alone my heart's special love: let there be none other save the High-king of heaven . . .

14   To the King of all may I come after prized practice of devotion: may I be in the kingdom of heaven in the brightness of the sun.

15   Beloved Father, hear my lamentation: this miserable wretch (alas!) thinks it time.

16   Beloved Christ, whate'er befall me, O Ruler of all, be thou my vision.[1]

Finally let us remember that when we use the word 'be' in this context, it is not so much a request as a fact. In many ways, when the writer says 'Be thou', we should say 'You are' and seek to realise it. Remember, we are not trying to make God come, we are seeking to open out our vision and see that He is already in His world and with us.

BE THOU MY VISION

Be thou my vision, O Lord of my heart.

———

I once worked in a coal mine deep in the Northumbrian earth. It had a strange atmosphere all of its own. But the most awe-inspiring thing was the darkness. It was so black when you turned your lamp off that you could not see your hand in front of your face. For a while in the area I worked there was no light at all except from the lamp fastened to my helmet. One day, while working on my own, I knocked the lamp hard against a stone and it went out. I was in total darkness with moving machinery near by. I hardly dared to move, only slightly backwards to the rough-hewn wall. It would have been easy to panic – or just to scream out – but I knew that very soon some fellow-workers would arrive. They would have lights and they would ensure that I was not left in the dark. I waited for what seemed an age – it was probably hardly five minutes. Then a light appeared. At first it was small and far away, like a pin-prick in the dark. But I knew it was coming in my direction. In fact, I could see three lights coming towards me. Soon my companions were attending to me, and in fact got the second bulb on my lamp working again.

It was not long after this, at New Year, that I heard for the first time:

> I said to the man who stood at the gate of the year: 'Give me a light that I may tread safely into the unknown.' And he replied: 'Go out into the darkness and put your hand into the hand of God. That shall be to you better than light and safer than a known way.'[1]

About then another quest began. I wanted to discover

a light that would shine in the darkness of the world –
something or someone that would give me a better
vision, in a world where the light seemed to be growing
dim.

It was a bit later that I became fascinated with a story
from the Old Testament. It is a story of the church
having grown old; visions were rare, the old priest was
almost blind. The children of the 'vicarage' had rebel-
led, as often seems the case. It seemed that the poor old
church had little to offer. If anything, it needed looking
after. Fortunately a woman saw that it was a place to
bring her son and leave him there. The boy looked after
the old man. At night he had to keep alert, to keep all his
senses tuned for a call or a cry. In listening for the other
person, the Great Other broke into his life. Perhaps he
would never have known this fact if it were not for the
old man, the custodian of the knowledge. Eli may have
almost lost his sight, but he realised it was the Lord
calling the boy. The nearly blind old man stood at the
dawn of a new day, and though the lamp burned low, Eli
handed on the light. He taught the boy Samuel to say,
'Speak, Lord, for your servant is listening'.[2]

I was to learn that those who listen carefully to others
are in the best position for hearing the Great Other. A
group of people in a similar state of awareness were the
shepherds on the Bethlehem hills. They had all their
senses tuned to the night and its movements. They were
open and receptive. While they were keeping watch,
the message came. But there was still a greater learning
to come, that the light had never been far away. The
Presence is always there. God is in His world and
seeking to break into our unawareness, to shatter our
blindness. In reality, neither we nor His world have lost
His Presence or His glory. But we have lost our ability to
see. We are like the man born blind and need pray,
'Lord, that I may receive my sight.'

There is a haunting song from the island of Harris in the Outer Hebrides. It was sung by a woman, a leper, who was an outcast from society, banished from her upland home to live on the seashore. Left alone on the fringes of the island, she discovered that she was not alone. Nothing could separate her from the immanent God, in whom she lived and moved and had her being. The transcendent had come down, God was incarnate in His creation, the Christ had come to Harris. In some strange way she knew this and was uplifted.

> It were easy for Jesu
> To renew the withered tree
> As to wither the new
> Were it His will so to do.
> > Jesu! Jesu! Jesu!
> > Jesu! Meet it were to praise Him.
>
> There is no plant in the ground
> But is full of His virtue,
> There is no form in the strand
> But full of His blessing . . .
>
> There is no life in the sea,
> There is no creature in the river,
> There is naught in the firmament,
> But proclaims His goodness . . .
>
> There is no bird on the wing,
> There is no star in the sky,
> There is nothing beneath the sun,
> But proclaims His goodness.[3]

She discovered, personally, that the Presence was 'not by conversion of the Godhead into flesh: but by taking the Manhood (and Womanhood) into God'.[4] In her own self she discovered 'the Word made flesh and dwelling among us', and she 'beheld His glory'. The light shone in her dark days. Her eyes had been opened and she shared the vision of the eye of the eagle.

Perhaps it is because we do not look often enough at the borderlands where worlds meet that we fail to discover what is beyond. We seem afraid of the shadows and the dark. We are unwilling to move out from our safe place. We do not like our securities or our ideas to be challenged. We are as afraid of a God that we cannot tame and control, as we are of being caught by the unpredictable in life.

There is much talk in church circles about God being within us, as though He were a possession. There is almost an implication that we are big enough to contain Him, and that He is only part of us. There is even the greater danger of suggesting that we can cage Him or control Him. It would be far more revealing to say that we are in God: 'In Him we live and move and have our being.' It is because we do not venture very far that we do not see that the God who is beyond is also the God who is near at hand. It is when we go out from the safe and secure, when we reach over new boundaries, that we discover the God who is immanent and yet in the beyond. We are ever so afraid to let go, in case we lose control: we are afraid to stretch out in case we cannot return. We need learn to 'let go and let God'. Let Him be the One who controls, for that is facing the reality of the situation. Let Him be the One who comes to meet us in our explorations.

There in the beyond, which is ever reaching to us, we discover a promise of an even yet greater potential, a richness that is still opening out before us. We see with the eye of vision even greater vistas, deeper relationships are waiting to be revealed. So we need to become explorers, that the vision of our world and ourselves may be extended. We need to discover the reality of our existence: to know who we are and to Whom we belong.

One of the great moments of our life is when we

suddenly have our eyes opened, and it is as if we see for the first time. We say with the blind man from St John's Gospel, 'I once was blind but now I see.'[5] Often we do not know how this sight or insight came about, but we do know that our vision has been extended. A prayer by Origen that I like using begins with the words, 'May the Lord Jesus touch our eyes, as He did those of the blind. Then we shall see in the visible things those things which are invisible . . .'

That is something which the Celtic Church seemed to do a lot more easily than we do today – 'to see in the visible things those things which are invisible'. I do not believe that they saw God in all his glory any more than we do, but they certainly saw signs of His Presence. They were aware of creation pointing towards its Creator, and because creation has a Creator we are offered a relationship through it to Him. They saw 'in scenes the unambiguous footsteps of God', to use William Cowper's words. For them, creation was a way of communing with God. Created things spoke to them of the goodness and love of the Creator who was involved in and with His creation. He was not a God who had left it to run itself. So creation was the means of communion with Father, Son and Holy Spirit. Everything spoke of a Presence, vibrated with His love. They saw a universe ablaze with His glory, suffused with a Presence that calls, nods and beckons – a creation personally united with its Creator in every atom and fibre. There was nothing in this creation that need be without, or was without, that glory. Through all things there was a chance of a personal relationship with God.

If it is not so for us, if our vision has become impaired, it is not that we are too materialistic, rather that we are not materialistic enough. We have limited our vision of matter, of God's creation. We need to discover again that there is no separation into sacred

7

and profane. We need to see that all is in God and that God can be seen in all. We need to forever extend our vision beyond that which we seem to set for ourselves. We need to regain a sense of wonder, reverence and awe. Teilhard de Chardin wrote:

> Happy the man who fails to stifle his vision . . . What you saw gliding past, like a world, behind the song and behind the colour and behind the eye's glance does not exist just here or there but is a Presence existing equally everywhere: a presence which, though it now seems vague to your feeble sight, will grow in clarity and depth. In this presence all diversities and impurities yearn to be melted away.[6]

Again he said:

> God whom we try to apprehend by the groping of our lives – that self-same God is as pervasive and perceptible as the atmosphere in which we are bathed. He encompasses us on all sides, like the world itself. What prevents you, then, from enfolding him in your arms? Only one thing: your inability *to see him*.[7]

This is the great tragedy of so many of us; our vision has become so restricted. One of our difficulties is that we are always wanting to take things apart, to analyse. To dissect living things is fatal! The Celtic Christians tended to seek to discover the underlying unity in things rather than their separation, to align things rather than to divide them. Instead of looking at secondary causes of secondary causes they were concerned with the Prime Mover who united all. There was a consciousness of the integral wholeness in nature, an almost tender awareness of the unseen strands that unite all things and that vibrate with the Presence.

So many of us have lost touch with this reality and

thus live in a fantasy world of distorted vision and great divisions. In this distorted world one can be very alone. This restricted world is of our own making and not half as exciting or interesting as the real thing. What we need to do is to break out from this narrow myopic world and widen our vision. Let us be seen as those who extend horizons, those who reach beyond the stars, beyond the created universe to the Creator Himself, who gives meaning and being to all. Let us look into the very centre of things and discover the mystery that unites all. Let us forever in our looking at material things say, 'Be thou my vision, O Lord.'

In the cartoon world I find Mr Magoo really funny; he is so myopic that he cannot see the end of his nose. Because of his lack of vision he is forever getting into scrapes. His near blindness leads him to all sorts of adventures of which he is unaware. He walks off a building just as a girder comes past, he steps off the girder as it touches the ground. He steps into an open manhole as a head pops out and acts like a stepping-stone. He walks across a lake stepping on the backs of crocodiles, thinking they are logs. His antics are hilarious. But in reality he is tragic; he would cause no end of trouble to himself and to others. In fact he would not survive for long, and neither would people around him. Where there is a lack of vision, life and communities are always endangered. Where vision is lost, people find their lives falling apart. It is of major importance to realise the need for vision and to take seriously the comment from the book of Proverbs: 'Where there is no vision the people perish.'[8]

Our vision of life and the world affects our being as much as our well-being. It is important to us that we have a clear vision of the world and ourselves. I remember once picking up a book entitled, *How to Improve your Vision Without Glasses*. It was a system of daily exercises. I cannot now quite remember the titles of each section but they were something like these:

> 'How to extend your vision'
> 'How to see what was once invisible to you'
> 'How to increase your range'
> 'Do not miss out on the small things, they are often important'.

I realised that nearly every chapter applied to me, not just to what I could and could not see but to my whole approach to the world. My vision had been far too limited. It reminded me of William Blake, who said: 'If the doors of perception were cleansed everything would appear to man as it is, infinite. For man has closed himself up, till he sees all things thro' narrow chinks of his cavern.'[9] Our world is never big enough to contain God completely; the bigger we see it, or the deeper into it we go, the better chance it has of giving us a glimpse of its Creator.

It is good to make the practical discovery that much of what we call 'spirituality' is in fact how we see. Our spirituality is our vision of the world, ourselves and our Creator. Without the vision of a Creator it is a very small and narrow vision indeed. That is why central to much of Celtic living and prayer is their vision of God, a God in their midst, a God who enfolds, a God incarnate, a God who encompasses the family, a God of the fireside and stable, God in waking and in sleeping.

The Celtic vision derives much of its insight from St John's Gospel, and the symbol of that Gospel is the eagle. The eagle was believed to be able to fly higher than any other bird and to see further. The eagle's vision was able to look deeper and to see beyond others, to see what for others was invisible. This was a very earthy vision, rooted in creation. The vision of the Celts was sacramental rather than mystical: they saw God in and through things rather than by direct visions.

Creation spoke to them of God, conveyed a Presence, because it was in God. When God spoke to them it was usually through His creatures. The Great Other communicated to them through others, through 'mouth of friend and stranger'.

The Celtic Church in its love for St John's Gospel sought to have this vision. They prayed that their eyes might be opened, that all their senses might be made alert to that which was invisible. They prayed that they might have the eagle's eye to see Him who comes at all times. They sought to discover Him in the garden like Mary Magdalene and to be able to say, 'I have seen the Lord.' Like the disciples in the Upper Room, they shared the joy of His Presence in their home, and received His peace. They expected to encounter Him when they were fishing and on the seashore, and they would be sure He shared a meal with them. Time and again they would express their love for Him like Peter and desire to follow Him forever like the Beloved Disciple.[10] They would say in their own words, 'We beheld His glory.'[11] They soared to the heights of awareness and saw deeper than many peoples, for they sought to see with the eye of the eagle.

Not only our vision but all our senses need to be re-educated and re-tuned. We are so used to belonging to a consumer society, which gobbles up one thing after another and savours very little. We need to sharpen our taste for living, and our listening to others. The Celt says we must take time to learn to play the 'five-stringed harp', that is, use all our five senses. Each of our senses can learn to respond to a wider range, and the very centre of our being to be allowed to vibrate to the call of Him who is. As God's world and revelation comes primarily through our senses, we need to be sure they are all functioning as well as can be. A person who is bad at listening to another is not very likely to hear the Great Other who is God. If our vision is narrow then there is no room for the great God. The road to the glory of God is through a reverence for and awareness of the glory that is all about us. If our attitude towards the world – or even towards a single creature – is wrong, then our vision will be distorted and our attitude to God wrong also.

A prayer for the day from Gairloch is about each of our senses:

> Do Thou, O God, bless unto me
>> Each thing mine eye doth see;
>
> Do Thou, O God, bless unto me
>> Each sound that comes to me;
>
> Do Thou, O God, bless unto me
>> Each savour that I smell;
>
> Do Thou, O God, bless unto me
>> Each taste in mouth doth dwell;
>
> Each sound that goes into my song,
>> Each ray that guides my way,
>
> Each thing that I pursue along,
>> Each lure that tempts to stray,
>
> The zeal that seeks my living soul,
> The Three that seek my heart and whole,
>> The zeal that seeks my living soul
>> The Three that seek my heart and whole.[12]

Through our ordinary – God-given – senses the Divine, the Holy Three, seeks out our heart and soul. If our senses are not aware of this they need re-training, until we are aware that we are part of the mystery of Creation. For many this will be like a homecoming. We shall discover that like the prodigal son we have been in a far country and living off poor fare – if not suffering from famine – when in our Father's house there are riches indeed. Like the prodigal we need come to our senses, for here is the road open to God. Let us also seek out our Father and say, *Be thou my vision.*

EXERCISES

1. Pray slowly, meditating on these words:

Open my eyes that I may see
The Presence that is all about me.
Open my ears that I may hear
The voice that is quiet yet ever near.
Open my heart that I may feel
The love of my God close and real.
Open each sense, make me aware
Of the Power and Peace always there.

2. Learn to pray, 'Lord that I may receive my sight.' (Mark 10.51)

or,

Teach me my God and King,
in all things thee to see . . .[13]

or again,

Wilt Thou not yield me vision,
Lord of Grace,
Of that vast realm
Of unhorizoned space
Which is Thy heart
That heart-room makes for all.[14]

3. Learn to see all things in God.
Seek first a reverence for all of creation. Everything that is, is full of mystery, is holy. Nothing is profane, all is sacred for all is in God. If we are to learn from the incarnation, we must learn that He is to be found in the most earthy and ordinary.

Seek him through creation.
See in the beauty of a sunset, a glimpse of the beauty of God.
See in the opening of a flower, the offering of a Presence.
See in the arrival of spring, a God who forever comes.
Hear in the call of a friend, the call of the Father.
Hear in the sorrow of the hungry, the voice of the Suffering One.

Hear in the words of the stranger, the Other calling to you.
Feel in the meeting of persons, that He is there in the
    midst.
Feel in the press of the crowd, a Presence passing by.
Seek to be more aware.

4. Isaiah described God as a 'hidden God' (Isaiah 45.15). But He is a God who wants us to seek Him out through contacts with His creation.

Seek Him in His works.
Seek Him in busy streets.
Seek Him in work.
Seek Him in silence.
Seek Him in outer space.
Seek Him within you.
Seek Him in church.
Seek Him in communion.
Know that all the time He waits to be revealed, for all is in
    Him.

Be thou my vision, O Lord of my heart.

LORD OF MY HEART

O Lord of my heart . . .
Great Heart of my own heart . . .

———

It was one of those beautiful blue sky days and the sea
reflected the blueness. The tide was going out and there
was a great number of people on the beach. The family
next to me were all occupying themselves, father was
reading the Sunday paper, mother was reading a book,
the little daughter was running backwards and forwards to the sea. One of those days when you feel you
want to respond to the words,

> The world is so full of a number of things,
> I'm sure we should all be as happy as kings.[1]

But there was trouble brewing. The little lass had
been going up and down to the sea with her bucket. The
tide had gone a long way out since they had arrived and
it left her sandcastle moat empty. All she was trying to
do was to fill it. No one explained to her the impossibil-
ity. No one took any notice of her great efforts. Backwards and forwards, bucketful after bucketful, all to no
avail. It ceased to be a joyful occupation. Each journey
took longer and became harder. There was a mounting
feeling of frustration, of emptiness, building up inside
the little lass. Suddenly, it broke out with a great wail.
'Aaaagh! Aaaagh! Aaaagh!'. The sound rose up and down
the beach. It entered mother as she threw her book
down; she now felt the same as her little lass. Father had
ceased reading, he was turning the pages of his paper
over and over in agitation, pretending not to be
affected. The frustration and irritation were reaching
out to others. I felt a great sympathy for this family, as I

also had more than once felt this emptiness. I know how impossible it is to fill certain holes that appear in our lives. The emptiness within can be no more filled with things than a hole in sand can be filled with buckets of water.

Every day, I see people rushing about trying to fill an emptiness: trying to fill every moment in case the void out of which they came returns. So many people dare not sit still, dare not have unoccupied moments. T. S. Eliot tells of this so well in 'Choruses from *The Rock*':

> The endless cycle of idea and action,
> Endless invention, endless experiment . . .
> Where is Life we have lost in living?
> Where is wisdom we have lost in knowledge?[2]

Yet perhaps they are right in avoiding stillness, for so many demons will turn up to fill the empty space. People do need to be filled with something. The German language has a telling word for this feeling of emptiness, they call it *Angst*. It is not just anxiety, it is a sort of heartache that is very difficult to cure. To fill or fulfil themselves so many seek to possess more, but it can be like pouring water into the sand – the more we get the more we seem to need. In fact, for some people, there is a strange formula at work: the more they acquire the more they desire; the more they achieve, the more they ask of themselves. Often amid so much success, 'the last state of that person is worse than the first.'[3]

We are sometimes encouraged to see ourselves in a great universe, where we are so small. There is a way of seeing this planet as a small speck of dust hurtling through darkness. In a brief moment of time we are on that speck, infinitely small, transient, frail and of very little account. Yet that is only half of the picture. No wonder so many people have life out of focus if that is all that they see and know. By itself this one-sided view is very depressing. But thank God there is another side. Experience tells us of this other side; we do have 'infinite longings'. Turn inwards and explore your own being, seek to understand why you are frustrated. In a world so full of things, seek to comprehend what is meant when a teenager says, 'I'm bored.' Seek to explore the 'inner universe' of yourself.

When we look inwards, we discover that we can take in great tracts of the outside world and not be filled or fulfilled. There is a sense in which the whole universe itself cannot satisfy us. Our inner being is itself an expanding universe and finite things do not have the capacity to fill it, for it is made to hold the Eternal. The only real cure for *Angst* is the Eternal. Without God all frustrates: with Him in us the whole world is changed.

The writers of our Scriptures often called our inner being 'the heart'. The heart is not just our feelings or passions, it is meant to describe the very centre of our being. As the heart is almost in the centre of our body and the driving power of our circulation, it is not too far from the truth to look at it as the centre of our life. But it is not just a physical centre, it is that upon which our whole being is based. The words 'heart' and 'soul' can be almost interchangeable as in Psalm 84: 'My soul hath a desire and longing to enter into the courts of the Lord: my heart and my flesh rejoice in the living God.'[4]

Whether it is 'heart' or 'soul' it is obviously the whole person that longs to rejoice in the Presence. The heart is that which makes us essentially who and what we are, it is the very core of our personality and our existence. The Celtic Christians talked of the heart in this way; they saw it as being the very essence of our life. They were familiar with the writings of St Augustine and they knew well the saying: 'Lord, our hearts are restless, until they rest in Thee.' They knew that our relationship to God

19

had to be an affair of the heart, of the very centre of our being. They were aware that we had to be in Him, our hearts had to rest in Him, if we were to find peace.

There is a lovely story of a Hebridean princess which expresses the relationship between God and the heart. The princess was renowned for her gentleness towards all of life. Needless to say such a gentleness is not possible if we are feeling frustrated. She was not possessed by things, and so was able to give much away. She had given food and shelter to one of the wandering saints. Before he left, he asked her,

> 'Tell me the secret of your exceeding gentleness.' At this the lady mused for long, her eyes downcast; then answered softly as one waking from a lovely dream, 'There is no secret – only – only I am always at His feet, and He is always in my Heart.'[5]

This relationship of heart to Heart can be seen again and again in Celtic prayers. There is a wonderful series of morning prayers by a crofter on Morar called Mary Gillies; here are two verses:

> I am giving thee worship with my whole life every
> hour,
> I am giving thee assent with my whole power,
> With my fill of tongue's utterance I am giving thee
> praise,
> I am giving thee honour with my whole lays . . .

> I am giving thee loving with my devotion's whole
> art,
> I am giving kneeling with my whole desire,
> I am giving thee liking with my whole beating of
> heart,
> I am giving affection with my sense-fire;
> I am giving mine existing with my mind and its
> whole,
> O God of all gods, I am giving my soul.[6]

Then there is a prayer that was said at the barring of the door and the putting out of the light. As the darkness descends the speaker puts his trust in God. As the door is barred against evil, as he seeks to close his home to oppression, he opens himself to the Lord of his heart. In this darkness He will be his light. In the silence he is not alone.

> No ill-doing come to me
> Through bar, door-leaf, or turned key;
> No oppression may I see,
> King of glory leading me.
>
> Light of lights take darkness' part
> From thy place into my heart;
> Spirit's wisdom music start
> From my Saviour in my heart.[7]

Not only did the heart find peace and protection through the Presence, the heart was able to sing because of it. Then in turn, by singing, the heart opened itself even more to the Presence. Through song in the heart the world vibrated with the joy of a close relationship with God. One of the things that we know about the Celtic Christians is that they loved to sing; they loved to let the words of their prayers surround them with sound and vibration. This was something very special to them, and they did not share it easily with those who would not understand. They took the Scripture seriously which says 'Sing and make music to the Lord in your heart.' In this resonant harmony every fibre of their being tuned in to the world around them and to their God within the world. They knew, within themselves, that discord was being done away and that all is one in Him.

My mother would be asking us to sing our morning song to God down in the back-house, as Mary's lark was singing it up in the clouds and as Christ's mavis was singing it in yonder tree, giving glory to the God of the creatures for the repose of the night, for the light of the day, and for the joy of life. She would tell us that every creature on the earth here below and in the ocean beneath and in the air above was giving glory to the great God of the creatures and the worlds, of the virtues and of the blessings, and would we be dumb.[8]

As the Lord filled their hearts, He was known to fill the universe. Through such singing, they maintained a feeling of well-being which was truly theirs. A fullness entered lives that knew emptiness: a richness replaced much of the poverty that was their lot. Life was still hard but they were not left to get on alone. Life and creed were one because they were one with Him. This was not so much an intellectual statement as an experience that welled up from their innermost being. There, at the very centre of their life, and at the centre of all things, was their God.

In the Bible there are over nine hundred and sixty references to the heart. There is no one single precise meaning; perhaps this is purposeful if we are talking about the centre of our being. The centre is not something that can be tied down in a living person. Sometimes 'heart' means the will, other times it is the emotions, or the memory, or our personality.

Whatever it linked with it was used to describe the ground of our being. If you enter deep enough into the ground of your being, there you will find the Heart of our own heart. Peter Toon writes:

Standing before him in the heart suggests an attitude of sincere openness in the very centre of our being, the place where Love creates love; further, the placing of the intellect (mind) in the heart means there is no opposition between mind and heart, for both are open to, and submitted to the Lord God.[9]

22

When we seek out the core of our existence, if we are not to become self-centred, we need to continue our seeking until we come to God Himself. I know I must not give up until I come to the 'great Heart of my own heart'. Then I will discover that I am in fact in the Heart of God. My love may be small and vacillating, but His for me is great and sure. I will learn that I have always been in my Father's house and heart, and that he has been looking for me with an everlasting love. Life is no longer full of *Angst* which distorts and disturbs my vision. Through the heart relationship, the vision is cleared and all things seem to speak of God. Through the heart being receptive, God is able to approach us through all of His creation.

Bless to me, O God, the moon that is above me.
Bless to me, O God, the earth that is beneath me.
Bless to me, O God, my wife and my children.
And bless, O God, myself who have the care of
   them.

Bless, O God, the thing on which my eye doth rest.
Bless, O God, the thing on which my hope doth rest.
Bless, O God, my reason and my purpose.
Bless, O bless Thou them, Thou God of life.[10]

This common union with God and His creation leads to an awareness of the Kingdom which is within. It teaches us that the Kingdom of God is ever at hand and waiting for us to be receptive to it. If the heart is open to Him, and the will seeks to serve Him 'whose service is perfect freedom', then the Kingdom of God has taken root within us. The Kingdom is always there in potential, waiting for us to accept the rule of the King. Wherever He is loved, wherever He is obeyed, His Kingdom comes on earth as it is in heaven: 'I find Thee throned in my heart, my Lord Jesus. It is enough. I know that Thou art throned in heaven. My heart and heaven are one.'[11]

The deeper discovery than our love for God is His love for us, that we are in the heart of God. Because it is the Almighty who loves us, 'nothing can separate us from the love of God in Christ Jesus'. It is this that allows men to venture on dangerous and troubled seas. When God is in their boat, who are they to fear? In the knowledge of God's love they are not afraid to go anywhere. They know they may never return home, but they are assured of an eternal home. They know they may be lost at sea but they know in their heart they are not lost eternally. Like anyone else they do not want to be separated from their loved ones, yet if it happens they know they will not be separated from the Love of God.

> What can afear
> With God the Father near?[12]

Once again the Celtic fishermen take the Scriptures at their word: 'Let not your hearts be troubled, neither let them be afraid.' The love of God dispels the darkness of fear. The same love is a protection against the storms of life or the greyness of a dull day.

> Though the dawn breaks cheerless on this Isle today, my spirit walks upon a path of light. For I know my greatness. Thou hast built me a throne within Thy heart. I dwell safely within the circle of Thy care.[13]

Once we discover that the centre of our being is centred in God, we discover that we shall not perish. To know we are loved and accepted by God is to know that He will be with us whatever happens. This does not mean we shall escape the storms and tempests of life, but it does mean we are never alone. It also means that, through Him and in Him, we shall not be overcome.

Great Heart of my own heart, whatever befall,
still be thou my vision, thou Ruler of all.

EXERCISES

1. Open up to God. Know that in calling upon Him it is not that He comes to you, for He is always with you, it is you opening to your heart to Him.

> *O Lord, my heart is ready,*
> *My heart is ready.*
>
> Creator of all, come to me.
> Let your Presence renewing be.
> *O Lord, my heart is ready,*
> *My heart is ready.*
>
> Saviour of all, come to me.
> Let your peace enfolding be.
> *O Lord, my heart is ready,*
> *My heart is ready.*
>
> Spirit of all, come to me.
> Let your power refreshing be.
> *O Lord, my heart is ready,*
> *My heart is ready.*
>
> I come to Thee, Holy Three.
> Let me rest myself in Thee.
> *O Lord, my heart is ready,*
> *My heart is ready.*

Know that in your reaching out for God, He comes to meet you. He has been waiting for you to turn to Him, so that He may enfold you in His love. He is the great Heart of your own heart.

2. Pray slowly and carefully:

> Almighty God,
> to whom all hearts are open,
> all desires known,
> and from whom no secrets are hidden:
> cleanse the thoughts of our hearts

by the inspiration of your Holy Spirit,
that we may perfectly love you,
and worthily magnify your holy name;
through Christ our Lord. Amen.[14]

3. For most of us, the great moment is not so much when we say we love God but when we realise that God loves us. Go over these thoughts again and again.

Know that God accepts you whoever you are.
God loves you.
God gives Himself to you.
God is in the very core of your being.

You are in the Presence of God.
You are in the arms of God.
You are in the love of God.
You are in the kingdom of God.
You are in the heart of God.

4. Say quietly and with confidence:

I, Lord, am in your heart.
Your Presence enfolds me.
Your Presence is Love.

As we are in God, we are in His love, His peace, His power. Let us learn to pray the above prayer many times a day, changing the final word to whatever of God's gifts we feel we need. Know that in His Presence these gifts are offered to you.

ALL ELSE BUT NAUGHT

Be all else but naught to me, save that thou art.

The world and time have a habit of bringing all things to nought. There is a sense in which nothing seems to endure. There is something about nature and the human being which does not last. This is expressed in the Psalms in such a phrase as 'God bringeth all men to nought'. The poet Shelley describes a fallen statue in the desert, with these words on its pedestal:

> 'My name is Ozymandias, King of Kings:
> Look on my works, ye Mighty and despair!'
>
> Nothing beside remains. Round the decay
> Of that colossal wreck, boundless and bare
> The lone and level sands stretch far away.[1]

In a world where dangers were all around, the Celtic saints realised more than many the fragility of things. They knew the dangers of travelling through mountain passes and over uncharted seas. They had few of the protections that the modern city dweller pulls around him, so they were more aware that all things come to nought. Even today this feeling of things not lasting is part of the Celtic heritage.

There is something in human nature that makes us all seekers. Whatever we achieve, we feel that we should be able to go on to other things. None of us can live for long off past glories. Most of us have this feeling that life can be improved on. We seek something that is still beyond us, an inner urge makes us explorers. Once we cease from exploration there is a feeling that life is beginning to atrophy. T. S. Eliot writes:

Old men ought to be explorers
Here and there does not matter
We must be still and still moving
Into another intensity
For a further union, a deeper communion
Through the dark cold and the empty desolation,
The wave cry, the wind cry, the vast waters
Of the petrel and the porpoise . . .[2]

The quest for the beyond, for the Pearl of Great Price, for the Holy Grail, for hidden treasures, is part of the literature of all mankind: the symbols may differ but the quest remains the same. In nearly every quest there is a desert to cross or a jungle to conquer, there are always untold dangers. Such a venture calls for heroes; in the end the villains are always sorted out! It is in searching that we grow, in triumphing over the desert that we shape ourselves and show what we are made of. When there were still other countries to be discovered, many spent their energies doing just that; the quest was geographical exploration. Today the quest has moved to outer space. But what does it profit us gaining a foothold on another planet if we have not explored and understood our own inner being? The danger with questing simply after territory is that we carry to it all that is within us; we take to the new place all our restlessness and our destructive urges. Tacitus saw this in the first century: 'They make a desert and they call it peace.'[3]

There is a noughting, a desert that we all carry within us. No matter what we put into this desert place, we still suffer from dryness, from a longing to quench our insatiable thirst. This desert seeks to grow, and encroach on all the territories we know. Some people carry it around like a great 'black hole', and anything that comes in reach is swallowed up and diminished –

sadly, there is very little that comes out of them alive. This desert or emptiness needs filling, or one day we will just become part of it; it will spread into all our life.

There certainly is a desert that is simply destructive. But there is also a desert that is creative, a place of transition, which needs to be crossed if we are to leave the old behind. Before the Promised Land is reached there are deserts to cross, before the Pearl of Great Price is obtained we have to sell all that we have. The Old Testament tells the story of desert people, and how in the wilderness places they found refreshment. In the desert Jacob had his dream of the Presence; Moses found the holy ground of the burning bush. The journey from slavery to freedom involves crossing the desert:

> Remember how Yahweh your God led you for forty years in the wilderness, to humble you, to test you and know your inmost heart ... He made you feel hunger ... Learn from this that Yahweh your God was training you as a man trains his child.[4]

In the New Testament, the wise men crossed the desert to come to Jesus. John the Baptist chose the desert as the birthplace of his ministry. Of Jesus, St Mark says that 'the Spirit drove him out into the wilderness and he remained there for forty days, and was tempted by Satan. He was with wild beasts, and the angels looked after him.'[5]

It is good to notice that it is the Spirit who leads Jesus into the desert, for the desert can be a positive place. Once emptied of any trivial pursuits – or false directions – there is a chance for a space to be made for God to work. The desert can be a place where life blossoms, but it is not a place to ignore. When we are unwilling to enter the desert, in a strange way the desert enters us. The deserts of the world are growing; a new aridity and dryness is entering into the hearts and souls of civilised people. If we refuse to empty ourselves, it is often because we are already afraid of the growing emptiness within. We feel we could not survive if we discovered that our inner being was in fact a nothingness or moving towards nothing. But it is when we fear the desert, that we are unable to venture; we put off the Promised Land to another age and another time. We are unable to enter into the heritage that is rightly ours and are forced to sing of a happy land that is 'far far away'. We dare not let go of what we have and so we remain impoverished.

Those who willingly enter the desert may discover with Moses that God is truly present, that the very ground of the desert is holy ground. Those who do not run away discover that

> The desert will rejoice,
>   and flowers will bloom in the wilderness.
> The desert will sing and shout for joy;
>   it will be as beautiful as the Lebanon Mountains
>   and as fertile as the fields of Carmel and Sharon.
> Everyone shall see the Lord's greatness and
>   power . . .
> Streams of water will flow through the desert;
>   the burning sands will become a lake,
>   and dry land will be filled with springs . . .
> There will be a highway there;
>   called 'The Road to Holiness' . . .[6]

It was this knowledge, that the desert could be an exciting place of discovery, that drove many of the Celtic saints out of their homeland. These men and women saw that they had to make space for God, or they were aware that God was forever making such a space and if they did not let Him fill it nothing else was able to do it fully.

Time and time again in the *Voyage of Brendan* we hear of saints who set out to 'find a wilderness in the ocean', a desert place where they could be alone and without all the normal supports. A place where God could be allowed to fill every moment of their day. A place where they could discover that the very earth they walked on is holy, and so in turn know that every place belongs to God. Such a place is Skellig Michael, a remote rock in the Atlantic, the peak of a mountain that sticks 210 metres out of the ocean, seven and a half miles from the coast of Ireland. On this barren land, hardly approachable in most weathers, beehive cells were built where their inhabitants might discover the holy ground in the wilderness. Let those who visit such places on a fine day in summer not romanticise them; these truly were, and are, testing places. Only true heroes or heroines could survive there for long. Only those who are content with God can be satisfied in the wilderness. Once God is known to be there and to be met, the desert blossoms.

This tradition of seeking a 'wilderness' was one of the regular actions of Celtic saints. Bede tells how St Cedd in AD 659 '... chose a site for the monastery among some high and remote hills, which seemed more suitable for the dens of robbers and haunts of wild beasts than for human habitation.' In the same tradition St Cuthbert went to the Inner Farne for the first time in 675. 'Now the island had no water, corn or trees, and being the haunt of evil spirits was very ill-suited to human habitation. But when the man of God came, he ordered the evil spirits to withdraw, and the island became quite habitable.'[7] In 669 St Guthlac left the monastery at Repton for the wild and undrained quagmire of Crowland. His biographer Felix tells us he chose 'a place which many men had attempted to inhabit, but could not settle on account of manifold horrors and fears, and the loneliness of the wide wilderness.'

It is interesting to find how many little places in Celtic lands are called 'Disert', 'Dyserth' or something similar, each describing a place where someone sought to be alone to reach or discover an ideal: all such places were the scene of spiritual battle or adventure – places where someone was willing to face the noughting of the world to find the glory of the Presence. These are places where beauty is found, great and lasting beauty. For until we find Him, we do not know where true beauty is. Beauty without God is also a thing that comes to nought. The true beauty that endures, is a Beauty that is found within.

The desert is not an escape from the world. Those who go to it to run away will bring their own demons with them. It is not the desert-dweller, or the pilgrim for the love of Christ, who is the escapist – it is far more often the tourist! Fewer and fewer places are available to escape to, there are fewer empty spaces and un-crowded shores than ever before. Every year another splendid hide-away is discovered and marketed, and so destroyed. In parts of our world we have destroyed peaceful villages and quiet islands forever by marketing them as places to escape to. To the perpetual tourist here are some salutory words from Seneca:

How can you wonder your travels do you no good, when you carry yourself around with you? You are saddled with the very thing that drove you away. How can novelty of surroundings abroad and becoming acquainted with foreign scenes and cities be any help? All that dashing about turns out to be quite futile. And if you want to know why this running away cannot help you, the answer is simply this: you are running away in your own company. You have to lay aside the load on your spirit. Until you do that, nowhere will satisfy you.[8]

So even the Stoic Seneca could see and experience the noughting of all places. He knew that if a person carried around a desert within, they would find it wherever they went.

St Antony of Egypt said: 'For the sake of Greek learning men go overseas . . . but the city of God hath its foundation in every seat of human habitation . . . the Kingdom of God is within.'[9] The desert fathers were not escapists. Anyone who thinks the desert is an escape should try it!

> The simple men who lived their lives out to a good old age among the rocks and sands only did so because they had come into the desert to be themselves, their ordinary selves, and to forget a world that divided them from themselves. There can be no other valid reason for seeking solitude or for leaving the world.[10]

In the main the desert fathers were not mystics, they were practical men, who organised themselves into what we would call co-operatives and took their surplus produce by boat to market. But, they made a definite decision not to be caught up in the decadent values of their times. Society is ever bent on conventional and transient values, it measures by material standards. It is hard to be your own true self if you are trapped in the perpetual round of doing what is expected of you. It is hard to be measured by worldly standards unless you have 'gained' or 'possessed' something. We find it hard to begin to understand that 'to become the greatest we have to become the least.' If we are to discover our hidden treasure, we have to be willing to let go of all else – 'Naught be all else to me save that Thou art.' Let us show that we believe our God is the God who created

37

out of nothing, and risk welcoming the emptiness. If we accept that God brings goodness and order out of chaos, we should be less afraid to venture. But also, let us be clear about our quest: to give up something for something far better should hardly be called sacrifice. If the quest is for the Pearl of Great Price, then it is worth selling what we have to get it. Let the world see that we are not so much giving up as choosing a better way. The words of St Antony that moved Augustine of Hippo should still have their effect on us: 'Let no one who has renounced the world think that he has given up some great thing . . . The whole earth set over against heaven's infinite is scant and poor.'

What the desert fathers and the Celtic saints did show was a richness of spirit amid their material poverty, a great sense of the eternal present in the passing of things transitory. They showed great poise at a time when many were falling apart. They carried within them a 'rest', an inner calm for which they became famous. This inner calm, *quies*, is about the peace that the world cannot give, the peace that passes all under-standing, the peace that is a gift which comes with the Presence of God. They heeded and trusted the call, 'Come unto me and I will give you rest.' It was not an escape from the storms of life, but a witness to the fact that we are not expected to face them alone. They sought to acknowledge that, whatever the troubles which beset us, we are not left alone nor forsaken. Far from being a place of impoverishment, the place of emptying can become the place where we are en-riched. It is here that we can discover true and lasting values, and more important, here that we come to rely on our God. Instead of being the place of frantic searching, it can be the place of rest and renewal.

We need to create the space that allows for the Divine, to make room in our lives, as the innkeeper made room in the stable – or He will be born elsewhere. It is only if we are willing to be alone with the Beloved that we can say we truly love Him. This will not decrease our love for the world for it is His creation; it will enhance it. It will not make us love our neighbours less, for we will see Him in them, and so respect them all the more. It will not diminish us as people but fulfil and enrich us. To leave behind all material things is to show that we want the heart-to-Heart encounter, and at the same time it shows that we know where our true riches lie.

Remember, it is the Spirit who leads us into the wilderness. He calls us to where He can court us to love Him: 'I am going to take her into the desert again: there I will win her back with words of love.'[11] Make space daily in your life, times of emptiness for Him to fill, times of silence to heed His call. Know that

> God our pilgrimage impels
> To cross sea-waste or scale life-fells;
>   A further shore,
>   One hill-brow more,
> Draws on the feet, or arm-plied oars,
> As the soul onward, upward soars.
>
> Beyond the hills a wider plain,
> Beyond the waves the Isle domain
>   With richness blest
>   A place for guest,
> Where God doth sit upon his throne,
> The soul by Christ nor left alone.[12]

In whatever situation you find yourself, learn to say these words of love:

Be all else but naught to me, save that thou art.

EXERCISES

1. Make definite spaces in your day; stop all that you are doing and pray quietly and slowly:

Drop thy still dews of quietness
till all our strivings cease;
take from our souls the strain and stress,
and let our ordered lives confess
the beauty of thy peace.

Breathe through the heats of our desire
thy coolness and thy balm;
let sense be dumb, let flesh retire;
speak through the earthquake, wind and fire,
O still, small voice of calm.

(J. G. Whittier)

2. The 5p exercise is a good way to meditate. I call it the '5p exercise', because each part can be described by the letter 'P':

PAUSE, PRESENCE, PICTURE, PONDER, PROMISE

PAUSE

Stop all that you are doing. Let yourself relax. See if you can feel the tension going out of your body as you let go. Gently put all troubled and anxious thoughts from your mind. Make a space in your life for something to happen . . . Make room for God.

Breathe slowly and deeply.
Know He offers you His peace . . . accept it freely.
Let go . . . and let God.

PRESENCE

Know that He is with you.
This is the main purpose of the exercise – to discover that in Him you live and move and have your being.
Speak to Him quietly and say,

You Lord are in this place
Your Presence fills it
Your Presence is Peace.

40

You Lord are in my heart
Your Presence fills it
Your Presence is Peace.

There is no need to do anything. Just accept that He is there.
Rest in His Presence as you would in the sunshine.
Immerse yourself in His peace and in His love.

PICTURE
Picture the scene from Psalm 42.1–2.
The young gazelle travelling the desert places, searching,
seeking for water. This has become her over-riding purpose:
without finding it she will die. She must not weaken or give up
in her search. Picture the finding, the life-saving waters. See
her drink deeply. See how she revives. Know that you are like
this and say:

> Like as the hart desires the water-brooks: so longs my soul
>   after thee, O God.
> My soul is athirst for God, yea even for the living God:
>   when shall I come to appear before the Presence of
>   God?[13]

See yourself seeking and finding Him.
Picture yourself coming through the desert to be refreshed by
Him.

PONDER
How long do you think that you can survive without coming to
Him who is the living water?
Think about the dry and arid areas of your life and know that
God is calling you through them.

PROMISE
That every day this week you will seek Him out.
That if any dry or arid spells come along when you feel like
nothing, you will especially call upon Him.

3. Know that in your desires for change God is at work, and
that God is seeking you more than you are seeking Him.
Maria Boulding invites you to discover this:

41

All your love, your stretching out, your hope, your thirst, God is creating in you so that he may fill you. It is not your desire that makes it happen, but His. He longs through your heart.[14]

THOU MY BEST THOUGHT

... O Lord of my heart ...
be thou my best thought in the day and the night,
both waking and sleeping, thy presence my light.

———

When at theological college, I was introduced to the
'hours', that wonderful rhythm of daily prayer. Kelham
followed the monastic tradition of the Divine Office: the
tradition of 'seven times a day do I praise thee.' So life
developed a regular rhythm where prayer was the main
impulse but balanced with work, study and recreation.
There was something about the regular saying of the
daily offices that entered into your whole being. You
might not be aware of every individual word but you
were slowly taking it all in and digesting it until it
became part of you and your life. Only later did I hear of
the ancient monasteries in Ireland and Wales, such as
Bangor, where perpetual praise was sent up. There was
never a time when the worship of the community in
their church ceased. They sought to 'pray without
ceasing', on a shift system; they kept prayer going in a
way that some industries keep their machines going. In
a sense it was not difficult once you got into the way of
the system, though many a monk obviously found the
recollection itself very hard. If you say similar things
every day it is difficult to give the words meaning. But
this is true of any relationship of lasting love. Here is
part of a lovely poem from a monk of the tenth century:

Shame to my thoughts, how they stray from me!
I fear great danger from it on the day of eternal
   Doom.

During the psalms they wander on a path that is not
   right;

They fash, they fret, they misbehave before the eyes
   of great God

Through eager crowds, through companies of
   wanton women,
Through woods, through cities – swifter they are
   than the wind . . .

Without a ferry or ever missing a step they go across
   every sea:
Swiftly they leap in one bound from earth to
   heaven,

They run a race of folly anear and afar:
After a course of giddiness they return to their
   home . . .

O beloved truly chaste Christ, to whom every eye is
   clear,
May the grace of the seven-fold Spirit come to keep
   them, to check them!

Rule this heart of mine, O dread God of the
   elements,
That Thou mayst be my love, that I may do Thy
   will . . .[1]

The last two lines let us into the secret of prayer without
ceasing. Such prayer is only possible if God rules our
hearts and is our true love. I listened with awe to tales of
saints who prayed for days on end, and thought it was
beyond my strength. I heard of Patrick saying: 'In one
day I said about a hundred prayers, and in the night
nearly the same so that I used even to remain in the
woods and in the mountains; before daylight I used to
rise to prayer, through snow, through frost, through
rain . . . for the spirit was then fervent within me.'[2] I
wondered how I would ever have such ardour in the
cold, in the dark mornings, if I would ever rise with
fervour. How could I learn to pray without ceasing?

Again and again certain phrases kept recurring: 'Lord of my heart', and 'the love of God'. I was beginning to be drawn by the cords of love. I no longer looked upon 'pray without ceasing' as a threat, for it simply meant 'love without ceasing'. Strangely enough, though this must involve the whole of my being I felt relieved. I now knew it was not beyond my strength or ability, if it was not beyond my desire. I felt that this was a great joy and a privilege, the call to love God without ceasing. Loving is more exciting than words, and demands of us much more than words. If you have seen or heard *My Fair Lady*, you may remember Eliza Doolittle getting really mad with her rather timid young suitor. When she wanted love, all he could do was talk about it. She sang:

> Don't talk of stars
> Shining above,
> Don't talk of love,
> Show me . . .

Through prayer and word, this is what God is calling out for us to do, to show Him that we love Him now. In a sense all that He asks of us is our love.

About this time I discovered *The Book of the Lover and the Beloved* by Ramon Lull. New doors were being opened for me.

> They asked the Lover where his love first began. And he replied, 'It began in the glory of my Beloved.'[3]

The love of God was attracting me to a new way of life. Later still I could sing with joy John Denver's 'Annie's Song' and apply the words to God:

> You fill up my senses, like a night in the forest,
> Like the mountains in spring-time, like a walk in the rain,
> Like a storm in the desert, like a sleepy blue ocean,
> You fill up my senses, come fill me again.[4]

47

Prayer without ceasing was living in a loving relationship with the Beloved, and discovering that such love changes everything. So a song from Andrew Lloyd Webber's *Aspects of Love* rang so many bells for me and for a multitude of people:

> Love, love changes everything,
> Hands and faces, earth and sky . . .
> Nothing in the world will be the same . . .
> Love will never, never let you be the same.[5]

Such modern songs as these sound like so many of the early Celtic prayers to God because they are all about love. We slowly learn that God, Himself gave us that desire. God first loved us, and in fact made us for His love. All our loving is in response to the love that He has for us. It is God who pulls at the cords of our hearts calling us to Him, wanting us to return home. It is God who has searched us out before we seek Him. It is God who has forever given us His love freely.

The love of God is unconditional, but it does call for a response. As He gives Himself fully, it calls for us to respond with our whole being: 'Love the Lord your God with all your heart, with all your soul, and with all your mind.'[6] It is a pity that some restrict this commandment to mere words in church. An eighth-century comment on 1 Thessalonians 5. 17 asks,

> 'What is prayer without ceasing? The answer is not difficult. Some say it is celebrating the canonical hours, but this is not the true meaning. But it is when all the members (of the body) are inclined to good deeds, and evil deeds are put away from them. Then, when doing good they are praying to God, that is they incline their eyes to what is good, as Job says, 'I made a covenant with mine eyes.'[7]

48

Cardinal Newman described prayer without ceasing in a different way:

> God has created me to do Him some definite service;
>
> He has committed some work to me which he has not committed to another,
>
> I have my mission . . .
>
> He has not created me for naught . . .
>
> If I am in sickness, my sickness may serve Him;
>
> If I am in sorrow, my sorrow may serve Him.
>
> He does nothing in vain. He knows what He is about.

Such love expresses the fact that God loves us whoever we are and whatever stage we are at. God's love does not cease, through it He seeks to bind us to Him. To express this love the Church has always been full of prayers; it is not by accident that they have often been called devotions. Perhaps some of the finest expressions of love to God come from the very earthy prayers of the Celtic Church, such as the morning devotions of Mary Gillies quoted on page 000. Even after hundreds of years we can still feel the love that pours out of them. There is a rhythm in their prayers that gave a rhythm to their lives, it is very much the rhythm of love. For this reason many of the Highlanders were very coy about being heard: these were words between the llover and the Beloved, not just for anyone to eavesdrop on.

> If the people feel secure from being overseen or overheard they croon, or sing, or intone their morning prayer in a pleasing musical manner. If however, any person, and especially if a stranger, is seen in the way, the people hum the prayer in an inaudible undertone peculiar to themselves, like the soft murmur of the ever-murmuring sea, or like the far-distant

eerie sighing of the wind among the trees, or like the muffled cadence of far-away waters, rising and falling on the fitful autumn wind.[8]

We are fortunate that so many of these prayers have come down to us. One of the finest and most comprehensive is the prayer of Mary Gillies from which I have already quoted. Some of her prayer may even be the last remnants of an ancient Celtic creed, remembered and handed down through personal or family devotions. In her croft or at the milking she would affirm the presence of God over and over and over. There was no formality in this, for it is a love song. Though the words are now written down, I am sure they would be often changed as she sang them. This is certainly not the theologically correct creed of Synods. But what use is it to us if we can define 'love' and not have loved, if we can make statements about God but not have known Him? This 'creed' is by someone who talks with God and knows Him, who knows He is 'the Father of goodness and love'.

O great God of all gods, I believe
That thou art the Father eternal of all life above;
    O great God of all gods, I believe
That thou art the Father eternal of goodness and
        love.

    O great God of all gods, I believe
That thou art the Father eternal of each holy one;
    O great God of all gods, I believe
That thou art the Father eternal of each lowly
        one . . .[9]

We would do well for ourselves if we added this prayer to our daily prayers, affirming over and over that we believe and that 'God is', affirming it not only with our lips but with our minds and in our hearts. Words of the lover to the Beloved – 'I believe, O God of all gods, that you are ... here ... present ... with me now.' Then it would be good to add to that statement, once it was part of our awareness and longing, 'I believe, O God of all gods, that you are the eternal Father of me ... the eternal Father of my family ... the eternal Father of my home ... the eternal Father of my workmates ... the eternal Father of this city ...'

Slowly but surely this brings us to discover the underlying love that is present in our universe, for all is loved by God, He made all things in love. There are no divisions into sacred and secular, there are no places where He cannot be found or people in whom He does not dwell:

> Chief and God of the hosts, I believe
> That thou art the creator and maker of heav'n on
>   high,
> That thou art the creator and maker of soaring sky,
> That thou art the creator of oceans that under lie.
>
> Chief and God of the hosts, I believe
> That thou art the creator and warper of my soul's
>   thread,
> Thou my body's creator from dust and earth-ashes'
>   bed,
> Thou my body's breath-giver and thou my soul's
>   domain bred.[10]

There is no division of body, mind and spirit. We must not give the impression that God is only interested in our spirit. God loves us as whole persons, not bits of us. He is as much concerned about our bodies and minds as He is about our soul. You cannot treat them separately for they all go together to make up the whole. If one bit of the body or one bit of the community suffers, all suffer, even though awareness of the suffering may be slight. Our world is a world where one thing is linked to another, nothing stands alone, nothing is

51

uninfluenced by other things and nothing that exists does not have some influence on the whole world. The world is not so much made up of individual isolated pieces, as it is of things that are interlinked and joined together. Perhaps this is part of the thinking that is behind so many of the Celtic interweaving patterns.

> Father eternal, Chief of mankind
> Enwrap my body and soul entwined,
> Safeguard me tonight in thy love shrined.
> The saints' aid tonight my shelter kind.[11]

There is not only a unity of all things upon earth, a unity of body and soul, but a common unity with the saints. There was a firm belief in the communion of saints – a belief that would be expressed many centuries later in such words as, 'All are one in Thee, for all are Thine. Alleluia!'

This is the same unity that is expressed in St Patrick's *Lorica*:

> I arise today
> Through the strength of heaven:
> Light of sun,
> Radiance of moon,
> Splendour of fire,
> Speed of lightning,
> Swiftness of wind,
> Depth of sea,
> Stability of earth,
> Firmness of rock.[12]

It is when we ignore this underlying unity that we do harm, not only to ourselves but to the world. It is when we divide things into sacred and secular that we suggest that some are loved and others are not. It is when we learn that God loves us and the whole world that prayer becomes a natural response to all that is around us.

Then the whole world is transformed, every action becomes a way of expressing our love. No deed is too mean or lacking in glory. No place is devoid of the Presence. If we so choose, we can be conversant with our God at all times. If we truly love Him, this will be our desire day and night. It will transform our hearts and our faces, if we will allow it. Such love (prayer) changes everything.

Be thou my best thought in the day and the night,
both waking and sleeping, thy presence my light.

EXERCISES

1. Here are two verses from different hymns by George Matheson (1842–1906). Use them as expressions of your love.

> O Love that wilt not let me go,
> I rest my weary soul in thee:
> I give thee back the life I owe,
> That in thine ocean depths its flow
> May richer, fuller be.

> Make me a captive, Lord,
> And then I shall be free;
> Force me to render up my sword,
> and I shall conqueror be.
> I sink in life's alarms
> When by myself I stand;
> Imprison me within thine arms,
> And strong shall be my hand.

2. *Pause* in the day. Pause in the Presence of God. Stop all that you are doing and say:

> You, Lord, are in this place
> Your Presence fills it
> Your Presence is love.

> You, Lord, are in my heart
> Your Presence fills it
> Your Presence is love.

Add more verses, just changing the last word of the first line.

As you pray each verse, picture the reality. Know that God is there, He is offering you His love and wanting love from you. *Picture* this exchange in each verse. Now *Ponder*, think about it. God loves you right where you are. Your love may be small, but His is great. Rejoice in the *Presence* of the Beloved. Then *Promise* that you will continue to make such little acts of love throughout the day. Whenever you get a moment, express your love for Him. So you will learn to 'pray without ceasing'. Know that, even when the words stop, the love continues.

3. Pray regularly this prayer by George Appleton:

Enlarge, my heart, God,
to the dimensions of your heart,
O limitless Love.
Let nothing be thought
common or unclean
which thou hast cleansed.
Let no one be thought
too exalted, so that
I only respect
but do not love.
Let nobody be regarded
as too humble, so that
I patronise or despise.
Let none be thought
as of little value
and written off,
For each is dear to thee
with his own potential
and his own hope
and his own heartbreak.
Let me say to each with thee,
'O man greatly beloved'
infinitely and eternally
dear to thee.
O Lord Love,
enlarge my heart
to the dimension of thine.[13]

BE THOU MY WISDOM

Be thou my wisdom, be thou my true word.

———

The Celtic Church was thoroughly biblical in its beliefs about God. The Bible was ever their main book of study. However they brought to the Bible some great insights of their own; their meditating on the Scriptures brought out certain positive images that become very noticeable in their teaching. There is no doubt at all that they were Trinitarians; prayers abound that express the 'Three in One'. Probably the best known of the Celtic prayers to the Trinity is the Hymn of St Patrick:

> I bind unto myself today
> The strong name of the Trinity,
> By invocation of the same,
> The Three in One, and One in Three.

There are many other Trinitarian prayers. They are often linked with baptism or with the blessing given by the midwife – this latter was probably a conditional baptism that was given in case the priest did not arrive before a child died. This was sensible in a time of high child mortality. It was a way of rejoicing in the presence of God in the birth of the child, and declaring that the child was immersed in the 'Holy Three'. From the moment of birth, if not before, the infant was enfolded in the love of Father, Son and Holy Spirit. The sacrament of the Church was not to make this Presence and love happen, but to be a visible sign that it is happening. The Celtic Church had no doubt that God was present and ever active and at play in creation. The following prayer concerning the Trinity belongs to prayers that express the threefold Presence:

The Three who are over my head,
The Three who are under my tread,
The Three who are over me here,
The Three who are over me there,
The Three who are in the earth near,
The Three who are up in the air,
The Three who in heaven do dwell,
The Three in the great ocean swell,
Pervading Three, O be with me.[1]

In our day and age we are so afraid of being pantheists, of declaring that God is in His creation, that we have relegated Him to somewhere far beyond us. For so many, God is a remote God, who has to be sought and brought from a long way off; even prayer has become like a long-distance telephone call. If only we could capture again the vision of God at work in His creation, what the Bible has often called the 'wisdom' of God or the 'word' of God. We need to discover that our God is close to us. If we are afraid of declaring that God is in things, let us at least be brave enough to say that 'all things are in God'. What is most important is to know that our God does communicate to us through His creation. One of the great exponents, in our time, of this communication is Teilhard de Chardin. Here is an example from *Le Milieu Divin*:

All around us, to right and left, in front and behind, above and below, we have only to go a little beyond the frontier of sensible appearances in order to see the divine welling up and showing through ... By means of all created things, without exception, the divine assails us, penetrates us, and moulds us. We imagined it as distant and inaccessible, whereas in fact we live steeped in its burning layers. *In eo vivimus*. As Jacob said, awakening from his dream, the world, this palpable world, which we were wont to treat with the boredom and disrespect with which we habitually regard places with no sacred association for us, is in truth a holy place, and we did not know it. *Venite adoremus.*[2]

The wisdom of God at play in the world, and the word of God in all creation, reminds us that God is ever ready to offer Himself to us. We are not left alone or without His aid. There is no time and no place where God is not. There is no time when, like an absentee landlord, He leaves or forsakes us. What prevents us from seeing Him is only our own lack of vision. We are like Jacob before his dream; the Lord is here and 'we know it not'.[3] It is time we awoke out of this sleep and declared that 'the Lord is at hand'.

This knowledge of God active in our actions, makes us courageous in our doings. It is not for nothing that the lack of fear is often expressed in the word 'confidence': confidence means 'with faith', that is, living in a vital relationship with our God. We walk with confidence for our God goes with us. Confidence also comes because we trust in God: whatever is going on in our lives, we believe that through Him all things work to the good. Many of the Celtic prayers that express this in a strong fashion, are connected with ships and seafaring. It is worth remembering how troubled the seas are around the Hebrides, for it gives these prayers even more impact. We need to picture these men sailing stormy seas, sometimes lost for days, battling against great odds, and sometimes perishing in the waters. These prayers are not romantic in approach, but a full facing of the situation, aware of the dangers and aware of His love. It is a pity that such ways of praying seem now to be lost to so many working people.

Because of this deep sense of the Presence, the Celts naturally rejoiced in the fact that 'the Word was made flesh and dwelt among us.' Christmas was not for them a one-off event, but something that was forever happening. Time and time again, they celebrated the coming of Christ into their dwelling. They lived often in small crofts and life was hard, but regularly from them came prayers and poems that say, 'We beheld his glory.' St John's Gospel was often the basis of their meditation. They used the images from this Gospel regularly in their talking of God and, even more important, in their talking to God. It is interesting to note that the Church that often talks to God needs a far more poetic language than those who just talk about Him. The lover always knows that the Beloved is beyond description. Yet to tell others of that experience the lover has to search for deep and meaningful words.

The Celts were not only aware of the depth of meaning in certain words, they were also aware of their history. They were aware that such words as 'Wisdom' and 'Word' had a very long and meaningful usage. When such words are used we have to allow them the time to vibrate with the experiences of the ages. The daily recital of the Psalms in the Celtic monasteries influenced much of their thought patterns.

> The word of the Lord is true: and all his works are faithful.
> He loveth righteousness and judgement: the earth is full of the goodness of the Lord.
> By the word of the Lord were the heavens made: and all the hosts of them by the breath of his mouth.[4]

> It is the Lord, that commandeth the waters: it is the glorious God that maketh the thunder.
> It is the Lord, that ruleth the sea; the voice of the Lord is mighty in operation: the voice of the Lord is a glorious voice.[5]

The Word of the Lord is Love, expressed in faithfulness and in right relatedness. The Word is about our relationship to God and His relationship to us. When the Word is later expressed as the 'Word made flesh', the Celt sees this as a challenge to all our relationships. This is what made Martin give his cloak to a beggar, what made Aidan give his horse away; for in the ordinary human flesh of another person they saw the Christ. The Celtic Christians took very seriously the statement of Jesus in Matthew 25, 'Inasmuch as you did it unto the least of these, you did it unto me.' The way we deal with each other is truly the way we deal with God. For the early Christians, hospitality was of extreme importance, for who knew when He would come to them 'in the flesh'? This awe towards others is expressed in an enigmatic poem about hospitality,

> O King of the stars!
> Whether my house be dark or bright,
> Never let it be closed against anyone,
> Lest Christ close His house against me.

> If there be a guest in your house
> And you conceal aught from him,
> 'Tis not the guest that will be without it
> But Jesus, Mary's Son.[6]

We need to take note of this – the Word, Jesus, is involved in every meeting with another person. 'Where two or three are gathered together, there am I.' Those two or three are you and whoever you meet with. The two or three can be a doctor and patient, a couple of lovers, a tramp on your doorstep, a secretary and their boss, or even a great group of people. Wherever there is a meeting of people, He is there. How much we need to sharpen our awareness of this coming!

It is the same Word that is in the world, and the world

overflows with His goodness. Psalm 29 suggests that creation itself is perpetually singing the praise of its creator. Commenting on this psalm, G. A. F. Knight says:

> We do not need to be a specialist scientist to be aware today that what we once thought to be dead matter is as truly alive as tigers and mice. We now know to speak of the particles of life as 'living organisms'. It would not then be out of place to suggest that even these strange elements are worshipping the Lord in holy array.[7]

This psalm is about the voice sounding forth seven times, corresponding with the seven days of Genesis. It begins with the 'many waters' like Genesis' 'great deep'. The voice of the Lord brings the elements out of chaos, the voice of the Lord restores order and balance. This voice is the 'Word of God'. The Word was far more than a mere sound, it had an active and independent existence. It was capable of doing things, it was active. If we feel we are where the action is, it is a very little move from there to be able to say, '. . . and the Word was made flesh and dwelt among us.'

There is one more thought pattern from the biblical period which we need to understand about the Word. There was a time when Hebrew was a forgotten language. The Old Testament was written in Hebrew but only the scholars knew it. The ordinary people spoke Aramaic; they were no more able to understand Hebrew than we would Anglo-Saxon. It is for this reason that the Scriptures had to be translated into the language of the people. These translations are known as the Targums. At the time of these translations, there was a great fear of talking of God in any earthly terms at all. The scholars were fascinated by the transcendence of God, the distance between Him and His creation. Therefore the translators did their best not to impute to

God any human characteristics, feelings or thoughts. Whenever the Old Testament spoke of God in human terms the Targums replaced 'God' with the phrase 'the Word of God'. For example in Exodus 19.17 the Targums read, 'Moses brought forth the people of Israel to meet the Word of God'; in the Hebrew Scriptures Moses brings the people out to 'meet God'. When Isaiah gives us that wonderful picture of creation, 'My hand has laid the foundation of the earth (48.13), the Targums make God more remote and make Him say, 'By my Word I have founded the earth.' The Word of God came to be used more and more to describe the presence or the actions of God in His world. But there was no doubt that behind this use of words the transcendent God was still at work in His world and within it. The very term used to keep the feeling of God transcendent was completely transformed in the phrase 'the Word was made flesh'. Because of this event the world would never be the same again.

To add to this, the Greek term for 'word' was *logos*. For them *logos* not only meant word, it meant reason. In St John's introduction to his Gospel these two ideas are interwoven. *Logos* means both the Word of God and the reason of God. I am sure it is not by accident that they come together in our hymn as wisdom and word:

> *Be thou my wisdom, be thou my true word,*
> *be thou ever with me, and I with thee, Lord.*

The Jews had a category of literature that has been called 'Wisdom Literature'. The Book of Proverbs belongs to this category. In Proverbs there are certain passages concerning wisdom (*sophia*) that make wisdom personified. Wisdom becomes a co-worker with God and an agent in creation: 'The Lord by wisdom has founded the earth; by understanding he has established the heavens.'[8] We can see that God's Wisdom and Word are very much the same thing: the Word is the light of men, and Wisdom is the light of men. Word and Wisdom become interchangeable: 'O God of my fathers, and Lord of mercy, who hast made all things by thy word and ordained man through thy wisdom'.[9]

Wisdom, like the Word, is God's creative and enlightening power. Wisdom and the Word cannot be separated for both are expressions of God at work, of God active in the world, and dwelling within us,

> BE THOU my wisdom, BE THOU my true word
> BE THOU ever with me, and I with thee, Lord.

This activity of God is expressed again and again in the Christmas events. There is a lovely Christmas poem from Flora Macdougal, a cottar on Barra, called 'The Lightener of the Stars':

> Behold the Lightener of the stars
> On the crest of the clouds,
> And the choralists of the sky
> Lauding Him.
>
> Coming down with acclaim,
> From the Father above,
> Harp and lyre of song
> Sounding to Him.
>
> Christ, Thou refuge of my love,
> Why should I not raise Thy fame!
> Angels and saints melodious
> Singing to Thee.
>
> Thou Son of the Mary of graces,
> Of exceeding white purity of beauty,
> Joy were it to me to be in the fields
> Of Thy riches . . .[10]

He who lights the stars, who comes down from heaven, allows us to share in His riches. It is He who is 'at play in creation', for He is the active Word of God. Though the Celts distinguished the Persons of the Trinity in the traditional roles of Creator, Redeemer and Sanctifier, they did not try to keep the clear divisions that so many of us need today. They rightly saw that there is an interplay of Persons, there is a dialectic at work. It is not a case of either this Person or that, it is more often a case of 'both . . . and'. So we find poems to the Word made flesh that can be applied to any member of the Trinity:

> The Child of glory,
> The Child of Mary,
> Born in a stable
> The King of all,
> Who came to the wilderness
> And in our stead suffered:
> Happy they are counted
> Who to Him are near.

> When He Himself saw
> That we were in travail
> Heaven opened graciously
> Over our head:
> We beheld Christ,
> The Spirit of truth,
> The same drew us in
> 'Neath the shield of His crown.

> Strengthen our hope,
> Enliven our joyance,
> Keep us valiant,
> Faithful and near,
> O light of our lanterns,
> Along with the virgins,
> Singing in glory
> The anthem new.[11]

There is no doubt that the last verse fits in with the Old Testament ideas of the Word and Wisdom of God at work. We could also attribute much of this work to the Holy Spirit. What is important is that we experience this activity of God ourselves, and that we become aware of God at work in His world. We discover a creation that is not 'finished' but is ever new and ever being renewed. Our God is deeply involved in the processes of our world and is there waiting to be discovered. Our relationship to the world and to each other, reflects our relationship to God. The Celts knew well the saying of St John: 'How can we say we love God whom we have not seen, if we do not love our brother whom we have seen?'[12] Nor can we say we love God if we hate His creation. If we do not love the world, it surely because we are unaware of Him who is at work within it. Let us seek to open up our vision to God who is truly at play in His world and learn to rejoice with God who is at play in His universe.

Be thou my wisdom, be thou my true word.

EXERCISES

1. Seek to know that at all times 'the Word is made flesh and dwells among us.' Say with St Symeon:

I know the Immoveable comes down:
I know the Invisible appears to me;
I know he that is far outside the whole creation,
Takes me within himself and hides me in his arms.[13]

See that He comes at all times and in all places, and that He comes often in human form.

2. In this world we are discovering how everything that exists is linked to everything else. Sometimes the links are there to see but more often they are to be sought out with great sensitivity. A holistic approach should be made to the world and not just to medicine. We need to discover that we are all part of one great whole. Seek to discover that God, Himself, dances in and through His creation, the very universe is dancing to rhythms set by Him: He is the Lord of the Dance. There is no place whatsoever where God is not, He is to be found everywhere in all His fullness. Seek not only to affirm the Presence but to experience it. Learn to join the dance of the Lord of the Dance. Seek to experience the dynamic movement of God in your life and in the world around you. Discover that you are part of the dance of God. Do not stop until you can say that you share in the dance of the Dancing God. Look again at some of the interlacing patterns in this book and see them as expressions of how our God interweaves Himself into our lives and our world. Take some time to think over these words from 'The Lord of the Dance'.

I danced in the morning
when the world was begun,
I danced in the moon
and the stars and the sun,
and I came down from heaven
and I danced on earth,
at Bethlehem I had my birth:

Dance, then wherever you may be;
  'I am the Lord of the Dance,' said he,
  'and I'll lead you all, wherever you may be,
  and I'll lead you all in the dance,' said he.[14]

3. Some of the early fathers described creation as the 'game of God'. Seek to discover the wisdom and word of God at play in and upon creation. Find out for yourself, that this hide-and-seek God waits for you to discover Him. Respond to the divine, to the numinous, that nods to you throughout creation. Let all your senses reverberate to His Presence. Let your taste, touch, smell, hearing and sight all seek to take part in this 'game'. Develop your sensitivities that you may be able to say, 'I have seen the Lord.'

THY PRESENCE MY LIGHT

Both waking and sleeping, thy presence my light . . .
be thou ever with me, and I with thee, Lord . . .
be thou in me dwelling, and I with thee one.

———

At home we had a pair of Sunderland pink lustre ware plates with religious texts. One said, 'Prepare to meet thy God,' the other had an eye painted on it and said, 'Behold Thou, God, seest me.' The first plate meant very little, for I wrongly put off any meeting with God until a far future time, even a future life. I did not think at that stage that I could encounter God in His creation or experience His Presence within my life. My God was a god of history and the past rather than a God 'in whom we live and move and have our being'. He was the God of Abraham, Isaac and Jacob but hardly the God I experienced to be alive and active in all that I saw and did. He was the God of Palestine and Jerusalem, but hardly the same God of Alnwick and Northumberland.

However, the other plate had a different effect upon me. It had the strange suggestion that I was not alone: there was someone – or something – keeping an eye on me! This plate, certainly, proclaimed a kind of Presence – so I was glad it was not in a room that I went into often. I did not think of the 'eye of God' with any idea of loving oversight and so, if anything, I sought to flee from the Presence of God. Like Jonah, I 'set out in the opposite direction in order to get away from the Lord'. I too was 'running away from the Lord'.[1] It would be years later that I would discover that my God was the God of my native land, that He was to be met on the moors of Northumberland and in its market towns. I was very slow to learn that my God promised never to leave me or forsake me. Slowly I discovered that there was no place where God was not, from Him was no hiding place. I would discover later still that in Psalm 139 some ancient poet had expressed the same feeling:

> Whither shall I go then from thy Spirit: or whither shall I go then from thy presence?
>
> If I climb up into heaven, thou art there: if I go down to hell, thou are there also.
>
> If I take the wings of the morning: and remain in the uttermost parts of the sea;
>
> Even there also shall thy hand lead me: and thy right hand shall hold me.
>
> If I say, Peradventure the darkness shall cover me: then shall my night be turned to day.
>
> Yea, the darkness is no darkness with thee, but the night is as clear as the day: darkness and light to thee are both alike.[2]

Yet along my journey, certain moments spoke strongly. I remember sitting in the cinema listening to Mario Lanza dedicating himself to service with the song 'I'll walk with God from this day on, His guiding hand will lead me on.' I was caught up in the heroics of it, of the adventure of walking in a brighter Presence than I had done before. The images on the screen had moved me deeply, if only for a few hours. I was moved to more heroics when I watched the film *Scott of the Antarctic*, that heart-stirring moment when Captain Oates walks out into the storm. I wanted to be heroic; like all lads I wanted adventure, to stretch myself and expand my world. I remember leaving the cinema, on a cold winter's night, and taking my coat and jacket off. I wanted to experience for myself, in my own small way, what those great men experienced. I was learning the power of images to move me. Later I would begin to understand what Professor Maritain meant when he said: 'If a man does not seek first of all for the secret of

74

the heroic, the work he does for the common good will remain of little value.'[3]

We need to learn to use our imaginations far more, to let them play on the great subjects of life. Our imaginations have a far more powerful influence than any sort of abstract thinking. We need to create far more concrete images of what we say we believe, and of what we want to achieve. All new action of necessity comes first from such vision or visualising. A new building cannot be built without someone visualising it and drawing up the plans. Any new step forward or new project has to start in someone's imagination.

The imagination not only helps to create a new future but it can make us more deeply aware of events that have happened in the past. In fact, without imagination it would be difficult to recall much of the past at all. More important still, it is our use of our imagination that makes the present vibrate with greater intensity. First, we must know that the imagination is different from fantasy. Fantasy is when we allow our imagination to run riot, when we leave the bounds of the possible, when we are in flight from reality. Yet at the same time fantasy and imagination are very close together. The wonderful thing about reality is that it is far more fantastic than anything we can dream up! If we do not find our world an exciting place it is a sign that we have allowed the imagination to become dull.

There is a lovely story about an actor and a bishop. Whilst the bishop was having small congregations and poor attendances at his cathedral, the actor was performing to packed houses night after night. To say the least the bishop was rather put out, and asked the actor how it was that such a thing could be. The actor's reply was: 'I talk about fantasy as if it were reality, you talk about reality as if it were fantasy.' Far too often the Church is caught out in this way: the great mysteries of

75

life are talked of with little imagination and so people are hardly moved. In church we are often called upon to explore the most exciting facts of the universe and we forget to give the reverence that is due.

The sad thing about most people is that they can see only the blatantly obvious or the problems of life, they rarely enjoy its mysteries. We need to realise for ourselves the great mysteries that are talked about. We need to take time to explore them and to enjoy them. We must learn to treat more things as mysteries to be enjoyed rather than as problems to be solved. Facts such as the Presence, the Love of God, the Peace which passes all understanding, are available to us and can be experienced by a right use of the imagination. These great truths are there for each of us to enjoy. Whether we choose to be aware of them or not, such great gifts are being offered to us. Thomas Merton compared this becoming aware to taking part in a 'cosmic dance':

> The more we persist in misunderstanding the phenomena of life, the more we analyse them out into strange finalities and complex purposes of our own, the more we involve ourselves in sadness, absurdity and despair. But it does not matter much, because no despair of ours can alter the reality of things, or stain the joy of the cosmic dance which is always there. Indeed we are in the midst of it, for it beats in our very blood, whether we want it to or not.[4]

We cannot escape from the Presence, we can only choose to ignore it or seek to enjoy it. To enjoy the Presence we must develop our imaginative powers, so that we may see the divine reality at work in us and in our world. We must take time to visualise what we assent to with our minds, and to visualise the importance this has for us. The choice is ours, and it is one we will have to make again and again, though the more we ignore the powers that are about us the duller our senses become. The people of the Hebrides, in their daily lives, tried to visualise their walking with God. They had a daily routine which they called 'The Path of Right':

> When the people of the isles come out in the morning to their tillage, to their fishing, to their farming, or to any of their various occupations anywhere, they say a short prayer called '*Ceum na Corach*', 'The Path of Right', 'The Just or True Way'.[5]

This visualising expresses not only the Presence but a joy at being in the Presence. If God was with them in their travels, then they were right to say that they walked with God: to say anything else was to be an atheist. Once you realise that you never walk alone, a new confidence and joy comes into your journey. Yet, perhaps, only the Celtic Church could express this joy in a jubilant shout, 'Ho, ho, ho!'.

> With God be my walking this day.
> With Christ be my walking this day.
> With the Spirit my walking this day.
> The Threefold all-kindly my way:
> Ho, ho, ho! the Threefold all kindly I pray . . .[6]

It is as you would expect, 'joy in the presence of God'. By seeking to visualise the Presence and express the joy, we can far more easily partake of it.

We have to begin to 'imagine' the Presence by creating images that are helpful to us. Perhaps for some, it would be better to use the word 'image' or 'imaging', in case they feel that 'imagine' is to do with fantasising. We must learn to create images of our God which help to show that He is truly present and ready to strengthen and support us. Images which say to us that God is at work now in our world, and with us.

77

If we lose this sort of vision, of imaging, then we are forced to fantasise about our abilities to cope. It is lack of understanding and lack of confidence that make us declare that we are self-sufficient, that we can stand on our own feet. It is also a very myopic vision that thinks we can stand for ever on our own. If we dare to become more sensitive, we will realise that 'the sea is so large and our boat is so small': that there are many things that can and will overwhelm us. But it is also possible at the same time to visualise that up to this point we have allowed Jesus to 'sleep in the boat'. We have allowed our God-awareness to lie dormant, and we need to awaken our visualising powers.

It is amazing how naturally this came to the crofters on the Hebridean islands. Their lives and their songs proclaimed a glory that we seem to have lost from the earth. There was no part of their lives from which they excluded the Presence; they seem to have 'rejoiced in the Lord always'. At the kindling of the fire they would pray:

> This morning I will kindle the fire upon my hearth
> Before the holy angels who stand about my path . . .
>
> God, a love-flame kindle in my heart to neighbours all,
> To foe, to friend, to kindred, to brave, to knave, to thrall.[7]

When working at the loom they would continue:

> My Chief of generous heroes, bless
> My loom and all things near to me,
> Bless me in all my busy-ness,
> Keep me for life safe-dear to thee.[8]

Or in the byre at the milking:

> Be blessing, O God, my little cow,

And be blessing, O God, my intent;
O God, my partnership blessing thou,
And my hands that to milking are sent.[9]

There was no part of the day or place that was to be devoid of the joy of the Presence; and when the darkness descends, an Isleman knows: 'There need be no twilight. A man has Christ. "Is He not the truth?" he whispered. "Is He not the light? Is He not the keeper of the treasure we seek so blindly?"'[10]

These may not be the right images for us, but do we know this Presence in our jobs around the house and in our daily work? We cannot capture God in any single image, or icon, we cannot cage Him by words, but for each of us there will be special images. Sometimes we will use one image for a while and then naturally move on to another. In the same way Moses had the experience of the burning bush, but he then went on to Mount Sinai; and of course he kept the image of the Promised Land ever before him. On his travels, he pitched a tent for his Companion each evening: the tent of meeting, a sign of the abiding love of God for the people. In all was the promise that God was ever with them in their travels and adventures. In all God assured them, 'My presence will go with you, and I will give you rest.'[11]

We must affirm and experience this promise, for it is to us, Emmanuel, 'God with us'. The whole earth is full of His glory. The word that we need for our times is not written in a book, though the Book can help. The Word we need is the Word made flesh, real, concrete, and dwelling among us. We need to discover again the mystery declared by Julian of Norwich: 'We are more in heaven than on earth.' Or by Thomas Traherne in his *Centuries*: 'Your enjoyment of the world is never right, till every morning you awake in Heaven; see yourself in your Father's Palace: and look upon the skies, the earth

79

and the air as Celestial Joys: having a reverend esteem of all . . .'[12]

Have you even tried to do this? Or to experience what Eckhart meant when he said, 'God created all things in such a way that they are not outside himself, as ignorant people falsely imagine. Rather, all creatures flow outward, but nonetheless remain within God'? This experience is there for those who seek it out. In fact, there is a sense that until these experiences becomes our experience the world is 'without form and void'. It is the Presence that gives fullness and shape to the world, the Presence that gives our lives joy and meaning. With the Presence come all His gifts. We cannot truly enjoy these gifts without the Presence, just as we cannot be aware of the Presence and not be aware of the gifts. With the Lord come His peace, love, strength. He offers Himself at this moment. It is time to stop talking about Him and to begin to talk to Him.

> Thy blessed unction from above
> Is comfort, life, and fire of love;
> Enable with perpetual light
> The dullness of our blinded sight.

EXERCISES

1. Seek to develop your imaginative powers. This is the 'Picture' part of meditation. Follow the advice of Ignatius Loyola, seek to use all your five senses. As a guide I have chosen the scene from the raising of the daughter of Jairus (Mark 5.21–4; 35–42). Read this passage of Scripture first, then:

Imagine Jesus and his disciples in their boat. Look at the scene as they step ashore, see the blue water, feel it as they step out of the boat on to the shingle. Can you smell the sea? ... Look at the crowds that have come to meet him. Listen to the hubbub of sound, hear the excitement: 'Jesus has come.' Feel the jostling as they crowd forward to be near him ... Now watch Jairus push his way through, see how some people make room for him. He is a well respected person, an official of the synagogue. People are curious, for it is not like him to push like this. Notice how anxious he is; look at his face – it is full of sorrow ... Listen to the gasp of surprise as he throws himself at the feet of Jesus. This is a real show-stopper, everything goes quiet ... Listen carefully to his words, hear the pain in them: 'My little daughter is very ill. Please come and put your hand upon her, so that she will get well and live.' ... See Jesus look at him and take him by the hand. He lifts him up. You may like to feel the strong grip of Jesus. There is great power in those hands ... Set off with them. The crowd is understanding, and excited, but they still slow things down. Jairus would have liked them to go faster ... Watch the people coming the other way; they are servants of Jairus. Feel the fear mounting ... Hear the cry of sympathy and sorrow as they say, 'Your daughter has died. Don't bother the Teacher any more.' ... Notice how Jesus hardly stops. He puts his arm around Jairus and says, 'Don't be afraid, only have faith.' ... We now see the mourners and hear their wailing. Listen to their mocking laughter as Jesus says that the little lass is not dead. There is a strange mixture of tears and hollow laughter ... Watch as the family, three disciples and Jesus go into the room. Go in with them. Feel its coolness, smell the spices. See the little girl laid out on her bed. She is only twelve years old.

Touch her face and feel how cold she is, the warmth of life has left her ... Watch Jesus bend down over her. See how gently he takes her hand in his. Listen as he says, '*Talitha koum.*' The tenderness and the actions give meaning to the words ... Watch as the little lass is raised by Jesus ... He keeps a hold of her hand as she walks ... Listen as he tells the family to feed her ... Rejoice with them that He was able to enter the 'other world' and to bring her back. Celebrate with them that He is the Lord and giver of life.

Now that you have done this, why not look at the missing part of the story? Read Mark 5.25–34 and use all your senses visualising it. The Celtic church called this form of meditation 'Playing the five stringed harp', because it sets out to use all our senses.

2. Here is an exercise in visualising the Presence of Jesus as done by Guy Brinkworth and described in his book *Thirsting for God*:

> As I work, a Loved Presence over my shoulder, as I drive, a Loved Passenger beside me. In my reading, cooking, studying, whilst teaching, nursing, accounting: in the maelstrom of the supermarket or waiting for the bus or train – ever the loving sense of a Presence, always that nostalgia for my Creator.

Take to heart the name of 'Emmanuel' – God with us – given to Jesus. Visualise its reality for yourself and others.

I often use this visualising when I pray for the sick. I know that God is with whoever I pray for, I know God loves them and is ready to care for them. I see the person as best I can. I enter the sick room or the hospital ward in my imagining. I 'see' the Presence standing there, and I know God is at hand. The person is surrounded by warmth and light. The sick one is held in love and hope. I know that God is there and active. Often it is our lack of vision that seems to keep Him out. In our visualising we are opening up channels through which God can work.

Now pick one individual who you ought to pray for and picture them in the Presence of God.

3. Here is a prayer from the Hebrides that sees God's Presence at all times. Pray it regularly with the use of your imagination:

God to enfold me,
God to surround me,
God in my speaking,
God in my thinking.

God in my sleeping,
God in my waking,
God in my watching,
God in my hoping.

God in my life,
God in my lips,
God in my soul,
God in my heart.

God in my sufficing,
God in my slumber,
God in my ever-living soul,
God in mine eternity.[13]

Or simply visualise:

Both waking and sleeping, thy presence my light . . .
be thou ever with me, and I with thee, Lord . . .
be thou in me dwelling and I with thee one.

THOU MY GREAT FATHER

Be thou my great Father, and I thy true son;
be thou in me dwelling, and I with thee one.

———

I watched a young lad and his father prepare to climb a rock face with a slight overhang. The boy was very young, perhaps even a little frightened, but very excited that they would ascend. The father was big and strong and obviously experienced. Before beginning the climb, the father reminded his son of the dangers and the need for caution. There would times when the son could not see him, but he assured the lad that he would be there. More than this, before they proceeded, the father bound them together by a rope and shackles. 'Now if you get into difficulties, I will be there and able to help you. Don't be afraid, you know how strong I am. I will not let you fall. Even in the worst bits, when you cannot see me, know we are joined together, you just need to give tug on the rope and I will respond. Don't worry about anything; I am there all the time, I won't let anything hurt you.' I watched them set off on this great adventure. The father knew the way and could have scaled it quite quickly but he set his pace to that of his son. The father led the way and they both began to ascend. I could see the confidence the father gave the son. I could see the father on the rock face even when the son could not. I watched them until they reached the top. What a wonderful relationship. What a wealth of images this event gave me.

It is good when we know that our safety and well-being are not dependent on our own strength, our own cleverness or even our own virtue. Our Father cares, and our well-being and safety are dependent on His presence and His love. It is of primary importance that we experience that loving relationship with God that is expressed in the word 'Father'. What matters is that we come to know for ourselves that He cares, He comes to us, He dwells with us and that He is 'mindful of us'. No matter what we have done or where we have wandered, He will welcome us home. It is He who will provide us with support and a new confidence. It is such a shame for us if we have lost sight of this, for then the darkness really threatens and there is no provision in the storms except our own feeble fantasies.

The age in which we live is hardly one of assurance or of awareness of the Presence. More than once, the modern person has been likened to an orphan on a lost planet. People genuinely feel alone in a hostile environment and with very little to guide them. In the twentieth century it seems that so many have lost any vital relationship with the Father. This is all the more reason for us to hold on to the reality of God as our Father. We must not let the images of the Fatherhood of God be lost through the confusion of the present age.

In his novel *The Castle*, Kafka portrays the loneliness and the confusion of our times. The main character, the surveyor, enters the scene without any relations or friends; he has no pedigree and no history, there is no story about his life up to this point. All he has is a letter of appointment as a land surveyor. The place he comes to is a small country town, with its shops, inns and streets. But like many of our newer estates there is no centre to it: the place lacks a heart. It would seem that there is no one who is really in control and no one who particularly wants to be responsive. There is a feeling that all have been dis-spirited. There is, for this reason, a difficulty about relationships – as a child of God, I am aware that when the relationship with the Father is broken, all relationships become more tenuous.

Over this situation broods the castle. You can feel that

the castle is there, that it is important and yet in some ways never quite approachable. This sort of feeling about community and about any God-like figure is very common today. Many have learned to survive without recourse to that 'hypothesis God', but they have hardly learned to live, and relationships seem to break down so easily. There is something about the fullness of life and the fullness of joy that eludes the times in which we live. So many of the communities in which we dwell are like that in Kafka's *Castle*. It feels like a place of famine and of impoverished relationships, and we know in our hearts that it ought to be better. We know that there is a richer way of living.

Jesus talked of such a situation in his story about the Prodigal Son (Luke 15). In seeking to become a possessor in his own right, the prodigal broke his relationship with the father. It was not that the father would not give, it was not that the father moved away. It was the son who was dis-eased; he was not at home in the present, he wanted to own things rather than to have this relationship. The son wanted to make himself the centre of his world. He had come of age and did not need a father. He was to learn by experience that because this relationship is broken, all other relationships break down also.

Francis Thompson expressed this alienation in 'The Hound of Heaven', a poem about man on the run from God. Here are some verse endings. The Pursuer tells the pursued:

'All things betray thee, who betrayest Me.'

'Naught shelters thee, who wilt not shelter Me.'

'Lo! Naught contents thee, who content'st not Me.'

and the final lines:

'Ah, fondest, blindest, weakest,
I am He Whom thou seekest!
Thou dravest love from thee, who dravest Me.'

The prodigal learned that you cannot buy love, it must be freely given or it is less than the genuine article. Soon his bought friends disappear. The richness of relationships gone, the son discovers the emptiness that is within, an emptiness that the land around him cannot satisfy. It is no use possessing things if you are empty inside. This is what Jesus implied when he said, 'What does it profit a man to gain the whole world if he lose his own soul.' Without the knowledge of being loved, life becomes bestial. To share pigs' food is about as low as the prodigal can be without dying. Yet within himself he knows the richness of home. He who was once sick of home carries within himself a homesickness, and nothing will satisfy him until he is home. We must note that his feelings are now about his father's house; his desire and prayer are not for forgiveness but for the father, not to receive something but to relate to someone. The longing is not so much to possess as to be possessed, to be loved. What he seeks is not the restoration of status but the restoration of a relationship. In his heart of hearts, he knows the generosity of the father. The other son would also have to learn that this love cannot be earned, or bought by being law-abiding, it is a gift that is freely given. This relationship is not gained by duty or worked for, it is of the heart, and can only be worked at. Love awakens reciprocal love. Relationships must be two-way in their workings.

Be thou my great Father, and I thy true son . . .
Great Heart of my own heart, whatever befall,
still be thou my vision, thou Ruler of all.

Vision is experienced as a homecoming; we see in depth the place we live in as we have never seen it before. In the Presence of the Father we have a new experience of love, of creation and of our own being. Like Moses, we discover that the place on which we stand is holy ground. Even though we may find ourselves far from home, and in a desert place, when we experience the Presence, we experience a homecoming. Fatherhood is about His availability to us. If we are willing to repent, to turn around, He is already there waiting to receive us. In love He waits for us to come: He has always been 'more ready to hear than we to pray'. He will travel the road with us, offering us His rest. Again and again the prayers of the western Highlands tell of the God who travels with us, of a Father who knows our needs and is ever ready to protect us.

> Thou King of moon and of the sun,
> Of the stars thou lov'd and fragrant King,
> Thou thyself knowest our needs each one,
> O merciful God of everything.

> Each day that our moving steps we take,
> Each hour of wakening that we know,
> The dark distress and sorrow we make,
> To the King of hosts who loved us so;

> Be with us through the time of each day,
> Be with us through the time of each night,
> Be with us ever each night and day,
> Be with us ever each day and night.[1]

Fatherhood tells us that God is not a god without feelings. He is not a god who made His world and then left it. He is at home in it and cares for it. God loves the world. In fact God so loves the world that He is willing to give Himself for it (see John 3.16). We must not narrow this love just to human beings. God's love is for the whole world and it is the whole world that waits in groaning for His redeeming love.[2] It is such a pity that so many Christians give the impression that we should not love the world. They portray God as a spoil-sport rather than a father. It is not just we that are His – 'The earth is the Lord's and all that therein is: the compass of the world, and they that dwell therein.'[3] One of the prerequisites of vision is that we love the world, and with some fervour and intensity. Love must always involve passion. In his book *Wordsworth and the Artist's Vision* Alec King wrote:

> What is necessary first for visionary power is an undaunted appetite for liveliness – to be among the active elements of the world and to love what they do to you, to love to 'work and to be wrought upon': to be 'alive to all that is enjoyed and all that is endured', to have the loneliness and courage to take in not only joy but dismay and fear and pain as modes of being without bolting for comfort or obscuring them with social chatter.[4]

To experience that the whole world belongs to God and that it is the Father's house, opens up a whole world of discovery. We discover that we are part of something far greater than we ever imagined: we may even begin to comprehend what St Paul meant when he said, 'to those who love God all things work for the good.'[5] All things work together. In God there is no division; in God there is an underlying unity. This is a unity that our world of broken relationships and the fractured universe need to rediscover. We can even discover this unity through looking at ourselves. God has used all of time, all of the world, to create us as individuals. We are linked by fine threads to everything else in the world. The relationship with creation, which we broke in our wandering, is restored when we come home to the

Father. We can then delight to know that God has made us from the minerals of the earth, and recreates us through the plants, the animals and the very air we breathe. We can begin to feel with St Francis that we are genuinely related to Brother Sun and Sister Moon. When we discover this, we learn that God has used these things to make us sons and daughters of God, and that He still uses these things to sustain us. 'St Patrick's Breastplate' expresses this in the verse

> I bind unto myself today
> The virtues of the starlit heaven,
> The glorious sun's life-giving ray,
> The whiteness of the moon at even,
> The flashing of the lightning free,
> The whirling wind's tempestuous shocks,
> The stable earth, the deep salt sea,
> Around the old eternal rocks.

Many of our problems about the greening of the earth, and ecology, have been created through our own insensitivity. We have lost sight of our roots and of our relatedness to all things. Nothing stands completely alone in this world, all things affect other things that are around them. If we have lost a love for creation, we cannot say we love its Creator. If we do not show respect for what the Father has in His house, we should not be surprised that we are not at home in His Presence, or in His world. Learn that God touches you through all of creation, that He offers himself to you through His world. He is truly incarnate in His world. In his 'Mass on the World', Teilhard de Chardin says it is the purpose of life to discover the union between God and his universe:

For me, my God, all joy and all achievement, the very purpose of my being and all my love of life, all depend on this one basic vision of the union between yourself and the universe. Let others, fulfilling a function more august than mine, proclaim your splendours as pure Spirit; as for me, dominated as I am by a vocation which springs from the inmost fibres of my being, I have no desire, I have no ability, to proclaim anything except the innumerable prolongations of your incarnate Being in the world of matter: I can preach only the mystery of your flesh, you the Soul shining forth through all that surrounds us.[6]

If the Father makes Himself at home in the world, so must we. At this stage of our life this is the only world we have got; if we do not appreciate it, then it is hardly proper to expect the Creator of it to offer us another at any time.

Fatherhood also expresses a personal care for each of us. We are His sons and daughters and He knows our needs. He is concerned about our provisions, about our daily bread. When it comes to food and clothing, our heavenly Father knows that we have need of such things. The God who clothes the grass and feeds the birds of the air, provides for us His sons and daughters. This love of the Father, though it is directed to the whole world, is deeply individual. He cares for each son and daughter individually. He calls each of us by name. 'The Lord said to Moses, I will do this thing also that thou hast spoken: for thou hast found grace in my sight, and I know thee by name.'[7] Or in Isaiah: 'I will give thee the treasures of darkness, and hidden riches of secret places, that thou mayest know that I, the Lord, which call thee by thy name, am the God of Israel.'[8]

There was a time when I tired easily of all those lists of names that you find in the Bible, I was not all that interested in who begat who. Now I know that every name is important; without that link in the chain the rest could not have happened. Someone may have seemed insignificant in their time, but without them the world would not be the same. You just have to look at the lineage of Jesus to understand that. Who would have thought that from some of those doubtful characters God Himself would come forth? God is interested in us individually.

As our Father, He has a personal interest in us:

> For only a penny you can buy two sparrows, yet not one sparrow falls to the ground without your Father's consent. As for you, even the hairs of your head have all been counted. So do not be afraid; you are worth much more than many sparrows![9]

This love, this Presence, this indwelling, is waiting for us to turn to Him, that He may fill our lives with goodness and peace. All that is asked of us is that we come to our senses, that we become truly aware that we are sons and daughters of God, that He is a personal God and seeks a personal relationship with us. Because this relationship is a living one, it is not static. It is a relationship that will grow, a relationship in which we are increasing more and more.

> He was in the world, and the world was made by him, and the world knew him not. He came unto his own, and his own received him not. But as many as received him, to them gave he power to become the sons of God . . . God himself was their Father.[10]

To return to the Presence is to enter into a new harmony with the world and to discover an inner peace. This peace is one that the world cannot give and that the world cannot take from us. It is personal, God dwelling in us and we in God. We will have a new assurance in the dark and a new hope for the future. We can express it like this:

I am serene because I know that thou lovest me.
Because thou lovest me, naught can move me from
my peace.
Because thou lovest me, I am one to whom all good
has come.[11]

I do not think that I shall fear thee when I see thee
face to face. For I call to mind my father, he who was
the true man and the kind. And my mother, the pure
one, out of whose heart flowed the waters of healing.
And, as I think of them, my pulses beat with joy and
cry to thee, Father, and say: 'Thou art more and
tenderer than they.' Therefore when I am come into
the court of thy presence I know that thou wilt look
upon me with my father's eyes and with my mother's
pity and thou wilt draw me to thy breast.[12]

Be thou my great Father, and I thy true son;
be thou in me dwelling, and I with thee one.

EXERCISES

1. Use the story of the Prodigal Son as a theme for meditation.

PAUSE

Stop all that you are doing.

Are you aware of where you are? Spend a little time just
opening up in awareness to what is around you.

Do you hear Him who calls you by name, who wants to
know you personally?

Are you responding to His love?

Be still now in His Presence, and let Him enfold you in His
love.

PRESENCE

Explore a little the fact that you are in His Presence.

Be aware that He is offering Himself to you.

Open your life to Him.

Do not talk about Him, talk to Him.

Enjoy giving yourself to Him as He gives Himself to you.

Say quietly: You, Lord, are in this Place.
Your Presence fills it.
Your Presence is Love.

PICTURE

See yourself as the prodigal son or daughter.

Using your senses, imagine you leave home,

taking with you everything you possibly can.

Do you see the tears in your Father's eyes?

Are you aware of the pain in His heart?

You never turn back – He watches until you are out of
sight.

Picture the good time, and the things you buy – including
friends.

But it does not last. Picture similar events in your life.

Now experience the hunger, shame, loneliness.

See yourself in the pigsty – know that you are far from
home.

Look back with longing to the happier times.

Turn around, seek to return, make your way home.

Long before home is in sight, He is there.

He has been longing for you, searching for you.
He runs to meet you with open arms.
He asks for no explanations.
He enfolds you in His love.

PONDER

Are you sure you have come Home and are not just after bed and breakfast? Think upon these words of St Augustine:

He who seeks from God
Anything less than God
Esteems the gifts of God
More than the giver.

Have you really come to Him, or are you just looking for a safe haven?

Do you want to be possessed more than to possess?

After having made the journey and been accepted – are you still staying outside? Though you are welcome, are you still at heart in a far country?

PROMISE

That you will seek to draw near to God – and let Him draw near to you.

2. Consider and visualise these words of Mother Julian:

He is our clothing, for love; He enwraps us and envelops us, embraces us and encloses us; He hovers over us, for tender love, that He may never leave us . . .

In this He shewed me a little thing, the quantity of a hazel nut, lying in the palm of my hand, and to my understanding it was as round as any ball. I looked thereupon and thought: 'What may this be?' And I was answered in a general way thus: 'It is all that is made.' I marvelled how it could last, for methought it might fall suddenly to naught for littleness. And I was answered in my understanding: 'It lasts and ever shall last because God loves it, and so hath all-thing its being through the love of God.'

In this little thing I saw three parts. The first is God made it; the second is that He loves it; the third that He keeps it.

But what is that to me? Insooth, the Maker, the Lover, the Keeper.[13]

Now choose some material object that tells you that He is its Maker, Lover, and Keeper.

Finally apply each of these words to yourself. Visualise what is implied when you accept that God is your Maker, Lover, and Keeper.

3. Grant us, O Lord, to awake out of sleep,
   out of unbelief, little belief, dull belief,
   out of death, into faith;
   and by hearing thy word,
        obeying thy will,
        doing thy works,
   to pass from darkness to light,
        from ignorance to knowledge,
        from blindness to sight;
   to move from repentance to pardon,
        from allegiance to love,
        from lethargy to power:
   And so, DECLARE THE FATHER,
        and thee, Redeemer Lord,
        and the holy and life-giving Spirit,
        one God, almighty, all loving,
        world without end.[14]

   Be thou my great Father, and I thy true son;
   be thou in me dwelling and I with thee one.

THOU MY WHOLE ARMOUR

Be thou my breastplate, my sword for the fight;
be thou my whole armour, be thou my true might;
be thou my soul's shelter, be thou my strong tower.

As a child I was given a set of model cowboys and
indians as a present. They afforded hours of enjoyment.
The cowboys symbolised for me the good forces and
the indians were the evil ones. Life was still at an
innocent and simplistic stage! When young friends
called, we always waged battles pitting one force against
the other. The dark forces were always given to my
friends; I retained the 'liberating powers'. But it did not
always work out as I wanted. Often the indians won.
Often the strategy of the opposing force was superior to
mine and I lost. I set about wondering what I could do
about it – I could not just lie back and accept defeat. I
saw what happened on the films, when an attack was
made on the wagon train, the cowboys made a de-
fensive circle with the wagons. Inside such a circle they
were safer, they had less chance of being defeated. But
there was a setback; I had one wagon, and you cannot
make a circle with one wagon. Still, Christmas was
coming. I could make a request and live in hope. On
Christmas day I was delighted, for I went one better
than a wagon train, I got what I had asked for, a fort.
Now the goodies should not lose, for they had a fort to
protect them. Though, I must admit, it was hard to make
any battle tactics if they did not come out of their
fortress. I wished that they could move their fortress
with them, that wherever they went they could still have
this mighty protection.

It follows on from a belief in a loving Father that He
will protect us in time of need. Because His love is an

everlasting love, it will not let us perish. 'God so loved the world that he gave his only begotten Son, to the end that all that believe in Him should not perish but have everlasting life.' God will offer us through His Presence a mighty protection. When the battle is fierce and the enemy forces strong, He is there to help us. Again and again this is declared in the Psalms. Probably the best known is Psalm 23:

> The Lord is my shepherd: therefore can I lack nothing . . .
> Yea though I walk through the valley of the shadow of death, I will fear no evil: for thou art with me; thy rod and thy staff comfort me.[1]

While at theological college, I said Psalm 91 every evening for five years, as it was part of the Office of Compline. Here was a promise of a Presence and a protection based on the 'most High':

> Whoso dwelleth under the defence of the most High: shall abide under the shadow of the Almighty.
> I will say unto the Lord, Thou art my hope and my stronghold: my God, in him will I trust.
> For he shall deliver thee from the snare of the hunter: and from the noisome pestilence.
> He shall defend thee under his wings, and thou shalt be safe under his feathers: his faithfulness and truth shall be thy shield and buckler.
> Thou shalt not be afraid for any terror by night: nor for the arrow that flieth by day;
> For the pestilence that walketh in the darkness: nor for the sickness that destroyeth in the noon-day.
> A thousand shall fall beside thee, and ten thousand at thy right hand: but it shall not come nigh thee.[2]

104

Some nights when it was dark and cold, and the day had been hard and troublesome, I knew that I still needed a fort. I needed something to shield and protect me, somewhere to go to regain strength and confidence, someone to support and comfort me. I was beginning to see that it was the Almighty I needed, to be my fortress and my might. It was not that I was wanting to escape the battle or to run from the enemy, I wanted to be as well clad as possible against the foe. I wanted to be able to stand as a man against whatever assaulted me in life. I felt that I was asking for a lot. But believing in the love of the Father, I was sure that in His own way, and in His own time He would offer me what was needed. I sought strength from the strong God.

The Celtic Church was very fond of the sign of the cross as a sign of God protecting against evil. Penitents were ordered to pray with arms outstretched in 'cross-vigil'. Columbanus advised his monks to mark their spoons with the sign of the cross in case the devil entered through their mouth – a protection against gluttony. There is a long prayer from the tenth century, entitled 'Christ's Cross'. The person who says it signs every bit of their body in turn with the sign of the cross, and in every direction. All was to remind them of the saving and protecting power of God. Here are some of the closing verses:

> Christ's cross over my community.
> Christ's cross over my church.
> Christ's cross in the next world;
> Christ's cross in this.
>
> From the top of my head
> to the nail of my foot
> O Christ, against every danger
> I trust in the protection of Thy cross . . .[3]

For those who used the sign of the cross it was not a charm, but an affirmation of their deliverance from evil. The cross is used as a sign of God's love and salvation. The cross is a reminder of His victory and that He will not leave us to perish. It is a pity that people are often afraid to use such a sign, for it is an acted out prayer and a statement about our faith.

It was much later that I came across 'St Patrick's Breastplate' and its expression of the protection that God gives to those who bind to themselves the power of God.

> I bind unto myself today
> The power of God to hold and lead,
> His eye to watch, His might to stay,
> His ear to hearken to my need.
> The wisdom of my God to teach,
> His hand to guide, His shield to ward;
> The word of God to give me speech,
> His heavenly host to be my guard.

What wonderful images of the attentive, powerful and protecting God! I began to say this prayer as part of my daily prayers. So I was amazed when I discovered the strange frontispiece to the copy of 'St Patrick's Breastplate' in the *Liber Hymnorum*, at Trinity College Dublin (folio 196):

Patrick made this hymn. In the time of Loegaire, son of Niall, it was made. Now the cause of making it was to protect himself with his monks against the deadly enemies who were in ambush against the clerics. And this is the corslet of faith for the protection of body and soul against the devils and human beings and vices. Whoever shall sing it every day, with pious meditation on God, devils will not stay before him. It will be a safeguard to him against all poison and envy.

106

It will be a defence to him against sudden death. It will be a corslet to him after dying.

Now there are some very strong claims there. We have to read it carefully, and make sure that they are not about magic and manipulation. If it implied that we made God do something, I would dislike it as much as I do the sticker which says 'Prayer makes God jump'. If a change is made, it surely must be in the awareness of the reciter. The claims are not really meant to suggest that we conjure up powers by the recitation of this hymn. But they do promise great things for us. They promise the protection of God; they declare the Presence and the power of God; they tell of a God who is with us and who cares for us at all times. The hymn does not make this reality happen, it seeks to make us aware of the reality. By meditating on the Presence, it seeks to open our sensitivities to the abiding love of God. It is amazing how blind we have become to this reality. There is a great need today to comprehend the reality of the grace we have already received. 'Our God is with us – so who can be against us?' declares St Paul.[4]

With the Presence come the gifts of grace: with the Presence come the presents, comes peace, comes love, comes light, comes life. None of these things are denied us, all are offered to us through Him who loves us and is with us. As I have already said, it is our imaging of this, our vision, that has become dull; it needs to be re-awakened and sharpened.

The early Celtic Church had many 'breastplate prayers', or '*lorica*', which declared the surrounding and encompassing of God. Such prayers were not to make God come – He is already there – but to open our eyes to the reality. Many of us are in the position of Gehazi the servant of Elisha, in that we do not realise what powers there are at hand to help us. When Gehazi was terrified by the forces that were against them he declared to Elisha, 'We are doomed, sir. What shall we do?' Elisha replied, 'Don't be afraid, we have more on our side than they have on theirs.' Then he prayed, 'O Lord, open his eyes and let him see!' The Lord answered his prayer, and Elisha's servant looked up and saw the hillside covered with horses and chariots of fire around Elisha.[5] I do not believe that Elisha created these forces, they were already there only well hidden. Being a man of vision he saw them, and helped such as Gehazi to see them also.

In breastplate prayers, the person who prays seeks to become aware of what is already a reality. We are acting like Elisha and praying, 'Lord open our eyes and let us see.' Such as in the prayer 'God be with me'.

God be with me against all trouble, noble Trinity which is one, Father, Son and Holy Spirit.

The bright holy King of the sun, who is more beautiful than anything to which we have a right, is a wondrous refuge for me against the hosts of black demons . . .

Against grievous oppression and all other cruelty may the Son of Mary graciously bless my body.[6]

It is when we lose sight of this reality that we are truly in trouble. The wonderful thing is that we are never left on our own, He is always with us. For many people in our world, it is not pain and suffering that are hard to bear, but the feeling that they have to be borne alone. One of the great tragedies of our time is all the lonely people. The good news is that total loneliness is a fantasy, for

Nothing can separate us from his love: neither death nor life, neither angels nor other heavenly rulers or powers, neither the present nor the future, neither the world above nor the world below – there is nothing in all creation that will ever be able to separate us from the love of God which is ours through Christ Jesus our Lord.[7]

It is sad that most people seek to live by the fantasy of their own creation rather than by the Presence and love of God. Such fantasy leaves us, our homes and our loved ones, greatly impoverished. The surrounding Presence and the encompassing love of God is something we need to rejoice in, for it gives dignity to our being; in it we know that we are loved and that we are children of God. Without this, all dignity is a hollow sham, and nothing is well. With this, no matter what happens to us, we can hear, with Julian of Norwich, God saying:

I will make all things well.
I shall make all things well.
I may make all things well;
and thou shalt see thyself that all things shall be well.[8]

This is something which, once we experience it, we know it cannot be kept to ourselves. The love of God includes all of His creation. If we experience something of the great love of God, we begin to know that it is all-embracing. God's love is not exclusive. He does not love some more than others. He loves you, no matter who you are, with an everlasting love. I like this little rhyme by Edwin Markham:

He drew a circle that shut me out,
Heretic, rebel, a thing to flout.
But Love and I had the wit to win.
We drew a circle and brought him in.

In their evening prayers the people of the Outer Hebrides sought to make known to themselves the surrounding of the love of God. They sought to be aware that they and their loved ones were ever under His protection. Their very prayer sought to show how deeply God loves and cares. The words that act as title for many of these prayers are telling in themselves: 'Protection Prayer', 'The Travel-shield of God', 'The Encompassing of the Three', 'The Compassing of God', 'Guarding of the God of Life'. Each deserves to be used regularly in prayer and meditation. Here is such a prayer for yourself or your family:

> The compassing of God be on thee,
> The compassing of the God of life.
>
> The compassing of Christ be on thee,
> The compassing of the Christ of love.
>
> The compassing of Spirit be on thee,
> The compassing of the Spirit of grace.
>
> The compassing of the Three be on thee,
> The compassing of the Three preserve thee,
> The compassing of the Three preserve thee.[9]

I like to use such prayers in ever-widening circles, knowing that God is with each and everyone I pray for, that He already loves them and offers Himself to them. When I pray for someone, I try to visualise the Presence, to see that God surrounds them and upholds them. Whatever is happening to the person, or whatever will happen, God does not forsake them, and in Him they will ultimately triumph over whatever is pulling them down. We must not lose sight of the fact that we are children of God, loved by Him, and inheritors of eternal life. It is because we have lost sight of this that we are in danger of despair.

Along with the prayer of encompassing, the Celtic Christians had a practice called the '*caim*', in which they drew around them a circle. Usually, they used their right index finger. Pointing outwards they turned, following the direction of the sun, until with their hand they had inscribed a full circle around themselves. This was a symbol of the encircling love of God. The person doing it believed that they were encircled and safeguarded from evil within and without. Making themselves aware of the encircling love had a deep, calming effect. Knowing that God was with them made them able to stand far more strongly. In the same way, through prayer, they encircled their family, their loved ones, their homes: they encompassed their work, their cattle, their croft. When words refuse to come, when we are in sickness, weakness or fear, it is good to act out God's love and care with our bodies. Make the sign of the cross meaningfully, or draw the *caim* around you.

> In the Name of the Three
> In the name of their might
> I will draw the ring
> That doth instant bring
> Safety from foes' affright.
> In the Name of the Three
> I shall rout all my fears,
> I shall stand all unscathed
> From the cast of their spears:
> Thus I shall know no overthrow.[10]

I watch a stormy sea, the great clouds rolling and waves mounting high; the wind is roaring and I can hardly stand up. Life has been hard. I have watched a loved one suffer and have been able to do little but be present. I feel as if, for a moment, I am going to be overwhelmed by it all. Lately, one thing after another has risen up and sought to swamp me. I am very much feeling mortal. I could do with some help to continue. Like the fishermen on the Sea of Galilee I send out a plea, 'Lord save me, or I perish.' I make the sign of His saving love. Then a new stillness comes, a deep calm that I have not known before. I know that You, Father, reach out to me in love. I know that You care. I know that You offer me strength and peace. Above all, I know that You offer me Yourself, and You are about me at this very moment. Now I am able to stand up and to walk tall. This is what confidence is, living and walking with faith. Confidence is having that special relationship with You; special, yet You offer it to each of us. Wherever I go, if the day be bright or great storms glower, I walk with dignity, for You, Lord, are with me. In my weakness, You are strong. In my troubles, You are peace. In my darkness, You are light. At all times Your love enfolds me and surrounds me.

Be thou my breastplate, my sword for the fight;
be thou my whole armour, be thou my true might;
be thou my soul's shelter, be thou my strong tower.

EXERCISES

1. Slowly and reverently make the sign of the cross. If you have never done it before – using your right hand, touch the top of your forehead, move down in a straight line to your solar plexus. Now touch your left shoulder and then your right. You may now like to cross your hands over your breast. Whilst you do this you may like to use one of these two ancient prayers, saying the words slowly and with deep meaning:

> We adore Thee, O Christ, and we bless Thee,
> Because by Thy cross and passion Thou hast redeemed
>   the world.

(With this prayer you may like to change the final word to 'me' instead of 'the world', or to 'my home', 'my family', 'my community'. It can become a very meaningful prayer for a variety of situations.)

> O Saviour of the world,
> Who by Thy cross and precious blood has redeemed us,
> Save us and help us, we humbly beseech Thee, O Lord.

Again, this prayer can be extended to include more than just 'us'.

2. Make the '*caim*'.

Draw around yourself a circle, using your index finger, going clockwise. If you are in a sickbed or in a busy office, you may only be able to visualise doing this. Do see yourself encircled. Then know that it is God's loving presence that enfolds you. It is His peace that surrounds you. Know that you are enclosed with His care. You may like to say:

> The Mighty Three
> My protection be
> Encircling me.
> You are around
> My life, my home.
> Encircling me
> O sacred Three.

Again we can change the fifth line to include anyone or any situation that we choose. Above all, be aware that you are acting out a fact: you are seeking to become more aware of Him 'in whom we live and move and have our being'.

3. You may like to read slowly, or meditate upon, Psalm 91. Picture each of the protections that God is for you. These are realities, think what they imply.

4. Learn to radiate the love of God.
   See yourself surrounded by God and His love. Make the *'caim'*.
   Rest awhile in that love . . .
   Let that love fill your life . . .
   Let it fill the place where you are . . .
   Know that your God goes with you . . .
   Visualise the day ahead . . . see that God's love is there, enfolding and surrounding every situation . . .
   See His love in ever-widening circles.
   God reaches out . . . He seeks to touch you . . . He encircles your loved ones . . . your home . . . your friends . . . your neighbours . . . your work . . . your travels . . .
   There is no place where God is not . . . Let Him work through you to make His love known. Radiate the love by which you are surrounded, know that it is reaching out in ever-extending circles.

GREAT POWER OF MY POWER

O raise thou me heavenward,
great Power of my power.

———

I had been given a bicycle. It was old, gearless and rather dilapidated, but to me it was a treasure. I believed I had boundless energy and could go anywhere. I cycled the four miles from Alnwick to the coast and back, it was quite easy. So with another twelve-year-old, for that was my age, I planned to cycle to Berwick and back. This was a distance of thirty-two miles there and another thirty-two miles back. Obviously we had not calculated what this would take out of us in terms of time or energy. We just said we were going out for a little ride and a picnic. By the time we arrived at the bridge over the river Tweed to enter Berwick, we were both fearful of our mistake. We knew then we had overdone it. We only just crossed the bridge and entered the edge of the town and turned around. We had come too far and knew we would need every ounce of energy if we were to get home safely. Legs ached and refused to work properly. I was exhausted, would soon not be able to go any further. My friend was very much in the same state, we were both ready to collapse.

About four miles out of Alnwick, I got off my bike and could not remount it. I could not even walk with it. Now I experienced for myself what the Chinese mean when they say, 'If you have a journey of a hundred miles, when you have done ninety-nine miles you are only half way.' I could not go on. No amount of will power would push on my tired limbs, I had gone too far. My friend left me and went on ahead. For the last few miles I had been too much of a drag on him. I was now alone, frightened and tearful. It began to get dark. No one seemed to

117

notice me. I thought I would die. Then suddenly, in his wagon, my father appeared. My friend had gone and told him of my plight. He got out of his cab and jumped down to me. He lifted my bike on to the back of the wagon. Then he lifted me into the passenger seat. Within minutes I was safely home and being cared for. I knew what it was to be loved and to be rescued when all my powers had gone.

This event would provide me with many images later in life. I knew what it was to have a father who would come out to meet me. I knew that when I was weary and powerless he came down to where I was and lifted me. I knew that I was not left alone, because I was loved. It was much later on that I came across a promise from God in Isaiah that suggested He would do the same: 'Even to your old age, I am he; and even to hoar hairs will I carry you: I have made, and I will bear; even I will carry, and will deliver you.'[1]

It has taken me a long time to realise that God does not need my support, rather it is I who need His. God does not need me to carry Him around, but there are certainly times when I need to be lifted by Him. I learned to pray each evening:

Support us, O Lord, all the day long of this troublous life, until the shades lengthen, and evening comes, the busy world is hushed, the fever of life is over, and our work on earth is done. Then, Lord, in Thy mercy, grant us a safe lodging, a holy rest, and peace at the last: through Jesus Christ our Lord.[2]

The request was to make me aware of the fact of the support and the uplifting power of God. So often in this life we are like a child with a load to carry, or a weighty burden to lift, we are dragged down by it. We strain and we stress, perhaps we sweat and we swear, but alone the burden is bigger than us, and we are unable to lift it.

We may with our own strength carry it for a good while, but it will get us down in the end. If we are adventuring there are times when we will find ourselves beyond our physical limits; if this never happens we really must wonder if we are trying to live life to the full. Once beyond those limits we discover that 'we have no power of ourselves to help ourselves'. We are not self-sufficient, even though we may like to give the appearance that we are. None of our powers are limitless, left to ourselves we run out of energies. We learn that we need help from outside, from a power that is greater than our power. Now, all the time the Father has been watching and waiting, wanting to help us. He has been calling to us and offering to help us. All we need do is to call upon Him and trust Him. He will carry our load for us. More than that – if need be, He will carry us also.

As another of my regular evening prayers I say, 'Into Thy hands, O Lord, I commend my spirit.' As the darkness comes, I commit myself to Him who is the light. I who have wandered all day, return home to the Father, and put myself in His keeping. I have also learned to pray this prayer whenever darkness or tiredness comes, whenever I feel confused or lost. Only recently I have started to use it at the beginning of the day. Too often I have gone on to the point of exhaustion, piling burden upon burden, before I call upon Him. Too often I have allowed myself to enter deep darkness before I have the sense to call upon the Light. I have suffered many 'deaths' before I have come to Him who is the Resurrection. There is a strange perverseness in us that prevents us from turning to Him, and making our homecoming. Though God calls, we still stall. It seems that He still comes unto his own, and His own receive Him not. This is expressed well in a modern poem:

I am the great sun, but you do not see me,
   I am your husband, but you turn away.
I am the captive, but you do not free me.
   I am the captain you will not obey.

I am the truth, but you will not believe me,
   I am the city where you will not stay,
I am your wife, your child, but you will leave me,
   I am that God to whom you will not pray.

I am your counsel, but you will not hear me,
   I am the lover whom you will betray,
I am the victor, but you will not cheer me,
   I am the holy dove whom you will slay.

I am your life, but if you will not name me,
Seal up your soul with tears, and never blame me.[3]

Let me remember, for all His Power God will not force Himself upon us. We must invite Him into our lives. We need to let His Power come to work on our power. We must allow Him who is the Resurrection and the Life to enter into our many deaths, that we may experience the resurrection now. We need to know that He comes to us so that we may have life and have it more abundantly.[4] This means letting Him enter the darkness and allowing Him to descend into our own hells. There are places in our lives where we all need Him to walk; we need His healing touch, His words of forgiveness, His liberating power. In the words of Gerard Manley Hopkins we all must

Let him easter in us, be a dayspring to the dimness in us.[5]

We must let Him transform our winter into spring, our darkness into light. Let Him come down to where we are and lift us up:

O raise thou me heavenward, great Power of
   my power.

Once again, this leads to the image of the Good Shepherd who is willing to lay down His life for the sheep, and who will go after that which is lost until He finds it. The Good Shepherd who is ever seeking those who err and stray. He it is who walks through the valley of the shadow of death. He is who descends into the dark: 'He descended into hell.' The Good Shepherd enters all the hells of this world, seeking out that which is lost, and we are promised that He will not give up until He finds it. In our very weariness is the call of God, who knows His sheep and calls them by name. He comes down to where we are. But He comes down that He may lift us up: 'And when he has found it, he lays it on his shoulders, rejoicing. And when he comes home, he calls together his friends and his neighbours, saying to them, Rejoice with me, for I have found my sheep which was lost.'[6]

The uplifting power of God is something to accept and rejoice in as part of His love. We need to know that He ascended so that we might also ascend: He rose so that we might also rise. George Herbert, in his poem entitled 'Easter' begins:

Rise, heart, thy Lord is risen. Sing his praise
Without delayes
Who takes thee by the hand, that thou, likewise
With him mayst rise.

It was for this that he came down, to lift us up. At the festival of the Annunciation the Orthodox Church has these words as part of Matins:

Today is revealed the mystery that is from all
    eternity,
The Son of God becomes the Son of Man;
Sharing in that which is lower,
He makes me share in what is higher.

Not long after writing down these words, I watched a practice rescue by RAF Boulmer in Northumberland. The helicopter was hovering over a very stormy sea and trying to maintain a fixed position. In the sea was a 'person' needing rescue. The waters were icy cold and the person in them would not survive all that long. The winchman was lowered from the safety of the helicopter into the cold North Sea. But it was for a purpose; he came down to lift up; he descended to raise the perishing to safety, to save them from death. I saw here a wonderful image of the incarnation, the resurrection and the ascension: 'Now that he ascended, what is it but that he also descended first into the lower parts of the earth? He that descended is the same also that ascended up far above all heavens, that he might fill all things.'[7]

He came down to where we are so that we should not perish. He came down to lift us up. When we are set in the stormy seas of life, He is also there, waiting and wanting to help us. So I can pray with Oscar Wilde:

Come down, O Christ, and help me! Reach thy hand,
For I am drowning in a stormier sea
Than Simon on thy lake of Galilee.[8]

Now I have an image of the disciples in such a stormy sea. Jesus has gone high into the mountains to pray, He wants to be alone, with the Father in prayer. The disciples are down below and travelling across the waters. For a while all is calm and bright – then the storm comes. Like many of the storms of life it is quite unexpected. Dark clouds and great waves descend on them from nowhere. Suddenly the disciples know they are in trouble and even they, with all their experience, feel powerless. But they are not alone, He sees their need. Jesus comes down from on high, down from where He was. He enters their situation, He goes into the storm. Somehow He walks in it and it does not defeat Him. It is His presence that brings a new peace. Such an awareness can make disciples foolish, Peter thinks he can do what Jesus alone can do, he tries to walk above the waves. For a little while it seems possible, and then, naturally, he begins to sink. What else would you expect? We can often ride out a storm, triumph over great waves; but not forever. Then Jesus reaches out. He who has come down lifts Peter up. Peter will not perish because he is not alone, so Peter will triumph over the waves.

Julian of Norwich had such an image in mind when she wrote:

> He said not: 'Thou shalt not be tempest-tossed; thou shalt not be work-weary; thou shalt not be distressed'. But he did say: 'Thou shalt not be overcome.'[9]

What a wonderful statement that is for us who are in the storms of life: we will not escape the storms in this world, but we need not be overcome by them. We are not offered an easy way out, but we are offered the Power to survive. Nor is this some impersonal power, it is the very Presence of God. Gerard Manley Hopkins expressed it in a different way:

> I admire thee, master of the tides,
>> Of the Yore-flood, of the years fall . . .
> Ground of being, and granite of it: past all
>> Grasp God, throned behind
> Death with a sovereignty that heeds but hides,
>> bodes but abides:
>
> With a mercy that outrides
>> The all of water, an ark
> For the listener; for the lingerer with a love glides
>> Lower than death and the dark . . .
> Our passion-plunged giant risen,

> The Christ of the Father compassionate, fetched in
> the storm of his strides.[10]

Once again Isaiah, who tells of a God who will carry, tells of a God who says:

> Fear not: for I have redeemed thee, I have called thee by thy name; thou art mine. When thou passest through the waters, I will be with thee; and through the rivers, they shall not overflow thee: when thou walkest through the fire, thou shalt not be burned; neither shall the flame kindle upon thee.[11]

Here is a God who gives power for our journey through life. Like Moses, we need to become aware of the Presence that goes with us, and that He promises to give us rest.[12] Once again we need get our imagination to work, so that we can appropriate for ourselves what is really being offered to us.

One of the ways the Celtic Christian did this was to have a series of journeying prayers. These can be seen as an extension of such statements as, 'Yea, though I walk through the valley of the shadow of death, I will fear no evil, for thou art with me.' Time and time again we need to affirm what is in fact the reality that is all around us. Too often we allow our vision to become fogged or narrowed; we need to re-tune to the Presence and Power about us. We need to know that 'as many as receive Him, to them gives He the power to become the sons (and daughters) of God.' Somehow we have to add the eternal to our perspective of life. It is for this reason that the Hebridean Christian prayed:

> God be shielding thee by each dropping sheer,
> God make every pass an opening appear,
> God make to thee each road a highway clear,
> And may he take thee in the clasp
> Of his own two hands' grasp.[13]

The Celtic Christians affirmed that they were always in the hands of God. No matter to what depths life descended, they knew that underneath are the everlasting arms. These hands that would bear them up, are the hands that bear the imprint of the nails. The Power-full God is a God of the passion and of compassion. He knows all the hells and torments of this world, so He is well able to come to our aid. He is there already, wanting to help us: He always stands alongside us, never leaving or forsaking us.

> God before me, God behind,
> God above me, God below;
> On the path of God I wind,
> God upon my track doth go.
>
> Who is there upon the shore?
> Who is there upon the wave?
> Who is there on sea-swell roar?
> Who is there by door-post stave?
> Who along with us doth stand?
> God and Lord on either hand.
>
> I am here abroad, without,
> I am here in want, in need,
> I am here in pain, in doubt,
> I am here in straits indeed,
> I am here alone, afraid.
> O God grant to me thine aid.[14]

Whatever our condition, our state of body or mind, He is the God who comes. He is the God who lifts us up, who rescues us from hell. Let us learn to come to Him and experience resurrection now. His Presence is a source of joy and of courage. Let us learn to say,

> *O raise, thou me heavenward, great Power of my power.*

EXERCISES

1. Learn to accept the gifts He offers with His Presence. Say slowly this verse from St Patrick's Breastplate, and mean every bit of it:

> I bind unto myself today
> The power of God to hold and lead,
> His eye to watch, His might to stay,
> His ear to hearken to my need.
> The wisdom of my God to teach,
> His hand to guide, His shield to ward,
> The word of God to give me speech,
> His heavenly host to be my guard.

2. READ
Read the story of the Lost Sheep (Luke 15.4–7).

RUMINATE
Chew the story over. See the sheep wandering off, getting further and further away. The night comes down and it is in a dangerous place. See the sheep slips over the edge of the cliff and on to a ledge. There is no way it can get back of its own accord. There are great briars that wrap themselves around it and trap it. The sheep will die there if it is left alone. Many have perished in such a spot. Already the shepherd has missed it and set off to find it. He calls it by name. The journey is long and dark. At last he hears its feeble cry. He has to descend the cliff where it has fallen. He has to go to where it is. The briars tear at his hands and feet, his head is also torn. But he goes on, he descends right into the mess it is in. He rescues it at great cost to himself. Some would say the sheep was not worth his effort – but he loves it. See how gently he lifts it. The journey back is slow and hard for the shepherd, the sheep is being carried. He comes back rejoicing and saying to all he meets, 'Rejoice with me, for I have found my sheep which was lost.'

REFLECT
See this as a mirror of yourself and your actions. You are the wanderer, you are the one who has got lost. You have 'erred

and strayed like a lost sheep'. Picture yourself in the ravine and in the dark. Know it is a dangerous place and that you cannot rescue yourself. You may even be in such a situation now. Listen in the silence and in the dark, for He calls His sheep by name. He is calling upon you. Let Him hear you respond. Call His Name. Repeat such words as 'Abba, Father', or 'Jesus, Saviour', or 'Spirit, Lifegiver'. Say these words over and over, knowing that He comes to you. Let the light enter your darkness. Let the Good Shepherd lift you out of where you are and bring you to a safe place. Rest in His arms and in His love.

RESOLVE
Resolve that you will not stay in the darkness, nor will you let yourself be trapped and alone. Whenever the darkness descends, promise that you will call upon Him who calls you by name.

3. Following the last idea of being lost and raised, you may like to use the words of Christina Rossetti:

> I have no wit, no words, no tears;
> My heart within me like a stone
> Is numbed too much for hopes or fears.
> Look right, look left, I dwell alone;
> I lift mine eyes, but dimmed with grief
> No everlasting hills I see;
> My life is in the falling leaf.
> O Jesus, quicken me.
>
> My life is like a faded leaf,
> My harvest dwindled to a husk:
> Truly my life is void and brief
> And tedious in the barren dusk:
> My life is like a frozen thing,
> No bud nor greenness can I see
> Yet rise it shall – the sap of Spring
> O Jesus, rise in me.[15]

4. PRAY:

O God, who knowest us to be set in the midst of so many and great dangers, that by reason of the frailty of our nature we cannot always stand upright . . . support us in all dangers and carry us through all temptations: through Jesus Christ our Lord.[16]

MY TREASURE THOU ART

Riches I heed not, nor man's empty praise;
be thou mine inheritance now and always;
be thou and thou only the first in my heart;
O Sovereign of heaven, my treasure thou art.

At the beginning of this century there was a sale at the vicarage where I live. Among the many treasures was a string of local pearls. These fresh-water pearls had been found in the river Esk in North Yorkshire. No doubt they were not easy to find. I wonder how many shells were opened and found without a pearl at all. How many weeks, months, or even years, had it taken to collect this string of fine pearls? Had the collecting been the ambition of one man or family? I only hope that somewhere this necklace is still valued, for it cannot be measured in money alone; I doubt if there is another like it in the world! I hope it still has pride of place among someone's treasures, that it is still worn and not relegated to some trinket box.

There was a time when our island was visited regularly by merchants seeking its treasures: jet from the Whitby area and pearls from our rivers, gold, tin and lead from our mountains. Even before Christ was born, merchants were making the journey from the Mediterranean, across dangerous seas, for the treasures of our land. These were men of discernment who sought out the best in the known world, and would not be fobbed off with something of inferior quality. They knew that their journey demanded that they did not waste time on inferior goods. They were not interested in baubles but in treasures. They were not captured by whatever came along, they were looking only for the best. They were seekers of beauty and quality and knew

131

that when they found what they were looking for it would not come cheaply.

Jesus tells the story of such a merchant:

> The kingdom of heaven is like this. A man is looking for fine pearls, and when he finds one that is unusually fine, he goes and sells everything he has and buys that pearl.[1]

The danger of our times is that we are encouraged to chase after too many things. By seeking to possess things we become possessed by them. By accepting attraction after attraction, our appetite proves to be insatiable. We seem to have lost the discernment that is able to distinguish between that which is trivial and passing and that which is of great worth and eternal. Such an attitude caused Oscar Wilde to remark that we 'know the price of everything and the value of nothing'. If we stop and think, too many of us want to say with Browning's Paracelsus:

> I had a noble purpose and the strength
> To compass it; but I have stopped half way,
> And wrongly give the first fruits of my toil
> To objects little worthy of the gift.

One of the biblical words for 'sin', simply meant 'missing the mark' – missing the target, like an archer whose arrow has gone astray, or a darts player who aims for double top and gets a one. Sin comes in, not because we are not able to hit the mark but because we have become satisfied with lesser goals. Sin is living below par when it is within our power to alter it. Most often this happens when we have lost our vision and no longer see where our true riches lie.

There is a story from the middle ages of a preaching friar who had long distances to travel. Because of this, a wealthy merchant gave him an ass on which to ride. It was with pleasure that the preacher set out on his next journey. When he arrived at the church he tethered the animal outside. But throughout the service his attention was drawn to the ass. Was it properly secured? Had he left it in a safe place? What if a thief had come along and had stolen it? This went on until the service ended, the preacher was all the time distracted. When he came out afterwards all was well, the ass was where he had left it. But he knew that a new danger had entered his life. He untied the ass, slapped its flanks and drove it off. Then he walked away in the opposite direction. He was heard to say, 'God forbid that my soul should be tethered to an ass.' He was determined not to give himself to a lesser purpose than was his aim.

The need to possess so many things is often a sign of a poverty within. There is nothing worse than being surrounded by worldly treasures and feeling that we are still poor and unsatisfied. If we measure a person's worth by their rate of pay, we shall be in trouble indeed. There is a richness available to us all, whether we have many possessions or none. In fact sometimes it is by giving away, or losing, what we thought was our security and treasure, that we discover our true riches. There is a lovely poem from tenth-century Ireland that deals with this subject. Marvan, brother of Gooary, king of Connaught has become a hermit. The king tries to woo him back to the court.

GOOARY: Why, hermit Marvan, sleepest thou not
               Upon a feather quilt?
               Why rather sleepest thou abroad
               Upon a pitchpine floor?

MARVAN: I have a shieling in the wood,
               None knows it save my God . . .

Marvan then in the typical fashion of so many Celtic hermits recites a great hymn in praise of all that is around him, of all the good things that God has given him. He ends with these words:

> The voice of the wind against the branchy
>   wood,
> Upon the deep blue sky:
> Falls of the river, the note of the swan,
> Delicious music! . . .

> In the eyes of Christ the ever young I am no
>   worse off
> Than thou art.

> Though thou rejoicest in thy own pleasures,
> Greater than any wealth,
> I am grateful for what is given me
> From my good Christ . . .
> Grateful to the Prince who giveth every
>   good
> To me in my shieling.

Gooary gets a glimpse of a more simple and satisfying world, uncluttered by possessions, and knows that his brother is rich indeed. The king's priorities are challenged by his poor brother. The poem ends with Gooary saying:

> I would give my glorious kingship
> With the share of my father's heritage –
> To the hour of my death I would forfeit it
> To be in thy company, my Marvan.[2]

Time and time again we see people of God meeting the challenge of Jesus – what does it profit a person if they gain the whole world and lose their own soul, or what can a person give in exchange for their soul? It is a comment on our times that we seem to be able to measure people only by success, by what they have gained, by the things that they have amassed, by the position they hold. It seems that the year has been a bad one if we end up with a smaller balance than last year. This all seems a far cry from Him who came down, the Lord who became servant of all, who was willing to 'give his life as a ransom for many'. There do not seem to be many disciples today who are willing to 'come down in the world'. Yet, perhaps, retaining the office of deacon in the Church suggests that we must be willing to come down and serve. We need to show that what the world counts as securities are not the really important things, as good as they are. Bede wrote of the Celtic saints of Lindisfarne:

> So frugal and austere were Colman and his predecessors that when they left the monastery there were very few buildings except the church; indeed no more than met their bare requirements. They had no property except cattle, and whenever they received any money from rich folk, they immediately gave it to the poor; for they had no need to acquire money . . . They were so free from the sin of avarice that none of them would accept lands or gifts for the building of monasteries unless expressly directed to do so by the secular authorities.[3]

We hear of Celtic saint after Celtic saint leaving all behind to answer the call of God. Time and again they set off for a new wilderness. Their very way of living was a challenge to the so-called securities of our world. Yet, in heeding the call to go out, they found the treasure that had been hidden. Something that had been buried within or by the debris of the multitude of things around them, was now set free. Quite suddenly their eyes were opened to the reality and they knew they had found the Pearl of Great Price. In his book, *Faith of a Moralist*, A. E. Taylor writes:

> It is just in letting go the cherished possession when the call comes, that we learn the true strength of the

personality, which can let so much go and yet survive, because it is not tethered. What we should really learn from these experiences is that there is that in our personality which is not fettered to any temporal good and can emerge enriched, not impoverished by the surrender of them all.[4]

For the Christian it is not just a matter of letting go, but of 'letting God'. It is not just negation and detachment but positive choosing and attachment. If anyone thinks that giving up things for God's sake is a hardship, let them heed the words of St Paulinus of Nola:

Think you the bargain's hard to have exchanged
The transient for the eternal, to have sold
Earth to buy heaven . . . ?[5]

The danger is that we are still tempted by the immediate, for it appears to be within our grasp. We act like Esau and are willing to sell our birthright for a mess of pottage, or to exchange the glory of the living God for a calf that eats hay. Yet the person who gives up all that he possesses for the Pearl of Great Price has the discernment to know that it is worth more than all he possesses. He is giving up the lesser for the greater. He is not being denied, but discovering that all he had hoped for is being fulfilled. Far from losing out, by the very fact he has found the great treasure, the person is enriched.

When I answered the call to the priesthood and set off for Kelham, I left behind a job with a future, a girl friend, an income (which would have supplemented my father's), freedom to come and go as I pleased, dances and the public houses. I was given a copy of the House Rule which included:

The fullness of sacrifice demands the sacrifice of all earthly goods. No Brother may therefore claim anything as his own, either for possession or enjoyment . . . While simple pleasures and enjoyments are

136

not forbidden, the life of all must be kept in real simplicity and poverty, and no one should have anything which he cannot willingly lay aside.

If you have given your whole life to God, why should you prefer to lose it in this way rather than that?

But I soon realised that the sacrifice was by my loved ones, especially as they supported me not understanding quite what I was up to. There was very little, if any, sacrifice on my part, for I was giving up something good for something better. I was discovering purpose and fulfilment; more, I was rejoicing in great mysteries and walking along the very edge of glory. I do not mean that there were not times of doubt and darkness. There were still times when I lost vision and felt like running away. But behind it all I experienced that God was seeking me even when I did not want to seek Him. Within me a richness of vision was growing. I saw that God loves me, even when I do not turn to Him. There is a lot of false talk about sacrifice. Such talk usually shows a lack of vision of what or Who we are aiming at. It still measures by the way of the world, which has a clouded and limited vision. We have not yet understood the greatness of God if we feel it is an imposition to have to seek Him out daily. The seeking is a grand adventure in itself: the finding is a treasure beyond description.

I was also beginning to discover that 'he who loses his life will save it': that the life I gave to God was given back to me, greatly enriched. God was not demanding a diminishment of me as a person, but fulfilment. I soon began to suspect any kind of Christianity that denied personality, that belittled the human being as a person. Anybody or any society that does not treat the person with the utmost respect should be looked at with great caution. There are too many systems and disciplines that work for their own sake – these it is good to renounce, or at least know that they alone will not satisfy! If I was being hollowed out, it was so that there was space for the Divine. If I was being emptied, it was so that He could fill my life.

I also discovered that the transient and the earthly are not taken away from us. We live in this world and we are part of it. At this stage in time it is the only world that God has put us in, and it is made by Him. To repudiate the creation means we cannot say a lot for its Creator. At this point I must say that I know it is a fallen and corrupt world, but it is a world that originally and ultimately belongs to the Creator. Christianity by its very nature is the most earthly of religions. Our God not only created the world but is incarnate within it. God is in His world. He is still to be found in stable and upper room, on the seashore or on the mountainside. He still enters the city and the sickroom.

The Pearl of Great Price is not so much a new thing as a new awareness. It is the opening of our eyes to the reality that is all about us – a reality that the Gospels describe as the Kingdom of God. We may have to travel far in our lives to find it, and yet all the time it is at hand and within us. We may have to go on and on seeking it, yet in some strange way we travel with it all round us. The Pearl that we seek is not a thing or a place but a Person, a Presence that never leaves or forsakes us. The radiance of this Presence is that which will change us and our whole world.

The attractiveness of God should counteract all baser attractions, in the same way that the merchant will give away his lesser pearls for the greater treasure. This is the relationship of love: we are willing to give all that we have because in so doing our life is filled by the Beloved. We give all to Him and He gives it back again transformed by His glory. If we give ourselves to things of lesser worth, it is because we have lost the vision of

138

the greater. In so doing we create a fantasy world, where values and securities are of our own making. We become like the man who built on sand and not on a firm foundation. Let Thomas Traherne call us back to a vision of the world which is where we live:

> For when you are once acquainted with the world, you will find the goodness and wisdom of God manifest therein, that it was impossible another, or better should be made. Which being made to be enjoyed, nothing can please Him more, than the Soul that enjoys it. For that Soul doth accomplish the end of His desire in Creating it.[6]

Perhaps you are overcome by the greatness of the world; you may prefer to take a single piece of God's creation and discover that it is full of the mysteries of His power and wisdom. So you will discover the treasure that is hidden and enjoy the world with a sense of awe. Thomas Traherne challenges us again: 'You never enjoy the world aright, till you see how sand exhibiteth the wisdom and power of God.'[7] By concentrating on the small things we often begin to realise that all is His and He has given it to us for our enrichment. There is no place or thing that is not in His Presence. As some delight in silver and gold, we delight in the glory of God. One more challenge from Thomas Traherne:

> Your enjoyment of the world is never right, till every morning you awake in Heaven; see yourself in your Father's Palace; and look upon the skies, the earth, and the air as Celestial Joys: having such an esteem of all, as if you were among the Angels. The bride of a monarch, in her husband's chamber, hath no such cause of delight as you.[8]

We need to rejoice and delight in that Presence, so that we learn to sing in our hearts:

Riches I heed not, nor man's empty praise;
be thou mine inheritance now and always;
be thou and thou only the first in my heart;
O Sovereign of heaven, my treasure thou art.

EXERCISES

1. 'Seek ye first the kingdom of God, and his righteousness; and all these things shall be added unto you.' (Matthew 6.33)
Ask yourself: What are your priorities?
Where does God figure in them?
Keep a log for a few days of how you spend your time. See what takes up most of your time. Write down how you spend your leisure hours as well as the working ones. Separate out what you believe are trivial pursuits from what is essential.
Think on the words, 'Where your treasure is, there will your heart be also.' (Matthew 6.21)
You may like to set in motion the words of William Cowper:

> The dearest idol I have known,
> What'er that idol be,
> Help me to tear it from Thy throne,
> And worship only Thee.

2. READ
Read the Parable of the Hidden Treasure. (Matthew 13.44)

RUMINATE
Think it over. How many people had crossed that field and never realised that it contained anything but soil? How many people had worked it with little reward? See the traffic going backwards and forwards over the years. They all undervalued the place they were in. No one was aware of the great treasure that was at hand. How often had this individual been in the field? What had changed? Perhaps he dug deeper than ever before, or was more aware of some sign that others had been blind to. Maybe he was on a new piece of ground, or he decided to turn it over for the first time. See his pleasure as he makes the discovery. He knows that it is worth all that he has, and more. He carefully covers it up again. Now he is ready to sell all that he has in order that he can obtain greater riches; he will get rid of the lesser to obtain the greater.

REFLECT
Jesus says that the Kingdom of heaven is like that treasure. The very Presence of God is waiting to be revealed to us and in us.

Have we still left these territories unexplored? Realise that the gaining of the treasure will not usually come cheaply. You might like to think over these words of Dietrich Bonhoeffer:

> Cheap grace is the deadly enemy of our Church. We are fighting today for costly grace.
>
> Cheap grace means grace sold on the market like cheap-jack's wares. The sacraments, the forgiveness of sin, and the consolations of religion are thrown away at cut prices ... Cheap grace is the preaching of forgiveness without requiring repentance, baptism without church discipline, Communion without confession ... Cheap grace is grace without discipleship, grace without the cross, grace without Jesus Christ, living and incarnate.
>
> Costly grace is the treasure hidden in the field: for the sake of it a man will gladly go and sell all that he has. It is the pearl of great price to buy which a merchant will sell all his goods. It is the kingly rule of Christ, for whose sake a man will pluck out the eye which causes him to stumble, it is the call of Jesus Christ at which the disciple leaves his nets and follows him ...
>
> Such grace is *costly* because it calls us to follow, and it is *grace* because it calls us to follow *Jesus Christ*. It is costly because it costs a man his life, and it is grace because it gives a man the only true life.[9]

REACT
Promise to seek that which is more precious; make sure life is not full of trivial pursuits.

3. Pray with George Appleton:

'I am as glad of thy Word
as one that findeth great spoils',
As a man stumbling on buried treasure in a field,
selling all that he has to buy that field;
As a man who knows all about pearls,
coming across one of priceless beauty
so perfect that he cannot be happy
until he possess it,
so sells all that he has

142

and with eager joy
buys that pearl;
As a young man with great possessions
desiring the deep quality of life
at last ready to give away all that he has
to enter the Kingdom of the Spirit
and make it the greatest
of his possessions,
his only treasure;
O God, I am glad, unspeakably glad
for thy Word and thy kingdom.[10]

THOU HEAVEN'S BRIGHT SUN

High king of heaven, thou heaven's bright Sun,
O grant me its joys after vict'ry is won;
great Heart of my own heart, whatever befall,
still be thou my vision, thou Ruler of all.

———

Once when I went camping with a group of friends I wandered off as the sun was setting. I walked a good distance and did not realise how quickly it would get dark. I found the journey back full of shadows and shapes. I was full of fears and beginning to feel that I was very much on my own and lost. The darkness began to close in around me. Everything looked very black indeed. I was now near to tears, with strong feelings of insecurity and inferiority to the powers around me. Then I saw it – a tent lit up in the darkness of the night. With a lantern inside, the tent glowed in the dark. I could see shadowy outlines of familiar shapes. I was not alone, I was among friends; their light was leaking through the tent to guide me to them.

It was years later that this experience of my early teens would help me to understand something of the 'glory of God'. I would hear about 'the glory being tabernacled amongst us': that God 'pitched His tent among us'. I wondered if, in the dark nights of the desert, the tent of meeting had a guiding light within it – a light that said that the darkness is being conquered, for God dwells with us. I felt that I began to see what Moses was aiming at when he had a tent pitched for God: here in their midst was an abiding Presence. When they travelled, this was a sign that the Almighty travelled with them. When the darkness descended, here was the pillar of fire to guide them. From such a place glimpses of glory were possible: here they no longer felt insecure or inferior, for a mighty Power was at hand.

Moving on to the New Testament, I realised that in Jesus, God has become tabernacled amongst us in a special way. 'The Word was made flesh and dwelt among us, and we beheld His glory.' For those with eyes to see, whose vision is cleared, in Jesus we get our clearest glimpse of the Divine. Not only is this a glimpse, it is the assurance that He dwells among us. We can also discover that he is the light that shines in our darkness; He is the light of the world. In the Advent season, as the days get dark, I thrill to the words of the blessing from the Alternative Service Book: 'Christ the Sun of righteousness shine upon you and scatter the darkness from before your path.' I know there is a play on words between 'son' and 'sun', and I like it; without either there would be no life for us. Both are the light of the world. Zacharias rejoiced in the coming of Jesus with the words, 'Through the tender mercy of our God ... the dayspring from on high has visited us, to give light to them that sit in darkness and in the shadow of death, and to guide our feet into the way of peace.'[1]

I was to learn time and time again, because He is tabernacled among us, that His Presence shines through His creation. We may only see through a glass darkly, but we do see hints of His being there, and glimpses of the Divine. There are times in our lives when our senses are cleansed, when we become more still, and we are aware of the great Other. We should learn to look over our experiences and say with awe, 'We beheld his glory ...' or with Jacob, 'Surely the Lord is in this place and I knew it not.' Perhaps, like Moses, we will have to devise a tent of meeting, a fixed place and a fixed time where we seek to get glimpses of glory. Here we will sit in quiet and, to use the words of John Donne, we can 'tune the instrument at the gate'. We need to train our senses so that they are more aware of Him who comes. Here at our tent of meeting we shall seek to 'let go and let God', we shall leave all aside to let Him fill our moments and our days. We shall seek rest from our striving and let Him be our power and our peace. Here we shall seek to speak to God face to face, as a man does with his friend. Here we shall look over our day to capture a vision of God in our midst.

Let it be said that most of us will not see God, but all of us can experience Him. If you read the book of Exodus chapter 33 verses 7 to 23, you will discover that what we have been talking about was experienced by Moses. For all the 'tent of the Lord's Presence' and the promise from God, 'I will go with you and give you victory', Moses asked to see the dazzling light of God's Presence. But he was told that a man can have only a glimpse of the Divine, for 'no one can see God and live'. What we are offered are signs of the Presence. The numinous is that which nods to us, that attracts us through and in Creation. It is a lovely thought that God is on a nodding relationship with us – and that He leaves signs of His presence for us to discover. The discovery may be only momentary, like a flash in the dark, but it gives us strength for our journey and hope for the future. Because I have travelled long dark nights on lonely roads, I am very fond of this description from Tom Stoppard's *Jumpers*:

How does one know what it is one believes when it's so difficult to know what one knows? I cannot claim to know that God exists, I only claim that he does without my knowing it, and while I claim as much I do not claim to know as much; indeed I cannot know and God knows I cannot. (*Pause*) And yet I tell you that, now and again, not necessarily in the contemplation of rainbows or new-born babies, nor in the extremities of pain and joy, but probably ambushed by some quite trivial moment – say the exchange of

149

signals between two long-distance lorry-drivers in the black sleet of a god-awful night on the old A1 – then in that dip-flash, dip-flash of headlights in the rain that seems to affirm some common ground that is not animal and not long-distance lorry-driving – then I tell you I know.[2]

How often I have seen that flash of lights without seeing a person, yet knowing that beyond the lights is a familiar friend or a fellow-traveller. The flashing lights are not the presence but a sign of the presence, and a hint of the greater Presence beyond. Again and again this Presence calls out through the multitude of things. The poets often speak of this Presence ever near and breaking into our lives. We can all experience with Gerard Manley Hopkins that:

> The world is charged with the grandeur of God.
> It will flame out, like shining from shook foil.[3]

A Presence can suddenly break into our darkness and shatter our blindness. This Presence is ever seeking us out, desiring to cure our deafness. Always wanting us to come home to the light and love of our Maker. Time and time again God calls and, so often, we are the one who stalls. But because He is ever near there is no hiding place from Him. The 'three person'd God' will continue to 'batter our heart' to seek admission. Often it is when we least expect it that the Presence breaks through. This was put forcibly in Robert Browning's 'Bishop Blougram's Apology'.

> Just when we're safest, there's a sunset-touch,
> A fancy from a flower-bell, some one's death,
> A chorus-ending from Euripides,
> And that's enough for fifty hopes and fears . . .
> As old and new at once as nature's self,
> To rap and knock and enter in our soul.

In a sunset, in a song, in a shop, in a saint, in the sun or in the Son, God seeks us out and draws us to Himself. I once felt this in a great congregation, the first time I heard Handel's *Messiah*. I was moved time and time again by the music and words. Great themes enveloped the church; passion and pain, pastoral love and peace all seemed to surround us and fill us. The air was vibrant and expectant, with a feeling that there was something else, something special, still to come. The enthusiasm of the singers was infectious. Suddenly we were all caught up in the rapture of the Hallelujah Chorus, praising the 'King of kings, and Lord of lords, forever and ever'. This proclamation echoed and reverberated all around us and within us. I wanted to be part of it, to join in. I felt that we were being allowed a glimpse of eternity, of the worship of God, of His Glory. We were privileged to be allowed a glimpse of the Divine.

Because of such awareness, and so many other experiences, of the God who nods to us, of the numinous, I know that life is enriched by such moments. I want others to discover it and enjoy it. This is not an experience for the privileged few but it is one we can all have. I want to repeat again and again, 'The Lord is at hand.' I feel I want to join Teilhard de Chardin when he says in his 'Mass on the World', 'I can preach only the mystery of your flesh, you the Soul shining forth through all that surrounds us.'[4]

The people of the Outer Hebrides managed to capture a feeling of this glory in so many of their prayers. Although these prayers are full of the doctrine of their beliefs, they well up from the heart and radiate out to all that is around them. There is not one area of life that is not touched by prayer and by the belief that He is there and He cares. So they begin the day with Him, and no matter what the day is like it will now hold a new brightness . . .

Though the dawn breaks cheerless on this isle
  today,
My spirit walks in a path of light
For I know my greatness.
Thou hast built me a throne within thy heart,
I dwell safely within the circle of thy care,
I cannot for a moment fall out of thine everlasting
  arms.
I am on my way to thy glory.[5]

The talking with, and singing to, God continued to give
glory to their day. They had prayers for fire-lighting,
walking to work, at work, in the home. They were never
without their companion.

Saviour and friend, how wonderful art thou!
My companion upon the changeful way.
The comforter of its weariness.
My guide to the eternal town.
The welcome at its gate.[6]

Such prayers are created by the joy of their inner
being, or are in fact the creators of that joy – a joy which
comes from having a glimpse of His Glory, from knowing that our God is tabernacled among us. Time and
time again, in the ordinariness of life, they rejoiced in
the Lord. They took to heart the words from the letter ro
the Philippians:

Rejoice in the Lord always; again I say, Rejoice . . .
The Lord is at hand. Have no anxiety about anything,
but in everything by prayer and supplication with
thanksgiving let your requests be made known to
God. And the peace of God, which passes all understanding, will keep your hearts and your minds
through Christ Jesus.[7]

Not only does our anxiety subside when we know
that we are not alone, but we get a new sense of victory.

We are able to triumph because we are not alone, we are not in the dark, we will not be defeated. Victory may not be yet, but through Him who loves us ultimate victory is offered to us. No matter what circumstances we find ourselves in, no matter how much goes against us, the final outcome is assured. The Christ Presence says to us, 'In the world you shall have tribulation; but be of good cheer, I have overcome the world.'[8] The whole of H. F. Lyte's hymn 'Abide with me' deserves a time of meditation on this subject: for the time being here is one verse:

I fear no foe with thee at hand to bless:
Ills have no weight, and tears no bitterness.
Where is death's sting? Where grave thy victory?
I triumph still, if thou abide with me.

This verse very much echoes St Paul in his writing to the Corinthians on the resurrection:

Thanks be to God, who gives us the victory through our Lord Jesus Christ. Therefore, my beloved brethren, be steadfast, immoveable, always abounding in the work of the Lord, knowing that in the Lord your labour is not in vain.[9]

Some of the great mistakes of our age are about life and its triumphs or otherwise. I believe in positive thinking – but some people are positively stupid in their affirmations. There are certainly times when 'mind over matter' will not work. There is a kind of so-called 'positive thinking' that refuses to accept the reality of the situation. In the way of our world every team cannot be a winner, nor can every individual. We have to accept that, left to our own devices, there is many a battle which we will not win. In our own right we are neither almighty nor eternal. However, when we link our lives to His, we can begin to predict the outcome with some confidence. We may seem to lose every stage of the battle, but we know we have not lost the victory. We may seem to go down at every round, but we know that we shall be raised at the last.

There were words of wisdom in an old soldier friend when, asked how he was, he replied, 'Battling on.' He knew that to win a minor skirmish was not to win the campaign. He knew that victory today did not guarantee that we would win again tomorrow. That old soldier when he died knew that, through his Captain, victory was assured him, but he had also heard the victory song many times:

And when the strife is fierce, the warfare long,
Steals on the ear the distant triumph-song,
And hearts are brave again and arms are strong.
                              Alleluia![10]

There are some very telling words at the end of Luke's account of the temptations of Jesus: 'The devil left him for a season.' This was not the end of the fight, it was but a single round. There was no doubt that the devil would be back. We must realise that as long as we live we are part of the 'Church militant here on earth'. We are not released from the warfare, but we are guaranteed the final outcome. We need to keep our vision of Him, and know that in Him we are more than conquerors.

We need to keep our vision of the other world or we will get this one out of perspective. J. Patterson-Smyth writing of the angels when Jesus was born in Bethlehem says:

Two worlds are in the picture. Keep the whole picture in view, else the story will go wrong . . . On the earthly side just a stable, a manger, the cattle in the stalls, a woman wrapping her baby in swaddling clothes. Nothing of wonder in it. Nothing of awe.

Until the world from which He came flashes in upon the scene . . . Remember it is all one story, all one picture . . . we believe in it all right. But we are dull and slow of heart. We let it slip out of view. And so our picture gets out of focus. Unless we keep habitually in mind that other world, that eager, interested, enthusiastic world, its very wonder and beauty tend to separate it from us, to make the picture of the angels from Heaven rather misty and cloud-like beside that of the manger and the Baby on earth. Now that must not be. Any haziness as to the reality and close presence of that world puts the whole story out of gear.[11]

We need to keep a vision of this other world. Not as a place far away or set in another time, but a world that keeps breaking into our lives. Not a world that runs parallel to ours, but a world that is closely inter-woven with ours, in fact a world in which our world shares and into which we can enter. We all need to set off on a quest, like Lucy in *The Lion, the Witch and the Wardrobe*, to discover a way of entering that other world and enjoying its great riches.

There is no need for us to be apologetic about this quest, or for that matter to apologise for our belief – those who do not believe have a lot more explaining to do. For the person with even the beginnings of vision, life is ever expanding with new vistas and horizons. True, we may be diminished like other folks, but we know we shall not perish: we may be knocked down but we know we shall not be counted out: 'The supreme power belongs to God, not to us. We are often troubled but not crushed; sometimes in doubt, but never in despair; there are many enemies, but we are never without a friend; and though badly hurt at times, we are not destroyed.'[12]

We know life to be a romance, because we know that all was created by love and for love. The relationships between God, the world, others, and ourselves, all offer contacts with mystery and love. In all there is an abiding Presence that gives meaning and purpose: without this Presence all becomes futile and hollow. If only we would allow our vision to be cleansed, then I am sure the words of the Stage Manager in Thorton Wilder's play *Our Town* would prove to be true:

We all know that something is eternal. And it ain't houses and it ain't names and it ain't even the stars – everybody knows in their bones that something is eternal and that something is to do with human beings. All the greatest people who ever lived have been telling us that for five thousand years and yet you'd be surprised how many people are always losing hold of it. There's something way down deep that's eternal about every human being.

We know that the 'eternal' in us is not ours by rights, it is a gift from God. In His love He does not want us to perish, as is our natural tendency, but to have – now – everlasting life. If there is a battle to be fought for eternal life, the outcome has already been decided in Christ our Lord. In Him we are more than conquerors. In Him a brighter dawn has broken. 'Thanks be to God, who gives us the victory.'

High King of heaven, thou heaven's bright Sun,
O grant me its joys after vict'ry is won;
great Heart of my own heart, whatever befall,
still be Thou my vision, thou Ruler of all.

EXERCISES

1. Seek to know that the Risen Lord, who descended into all
the hells of this world, has conquered death, and that He is
with you. Use the following hymn as a meditation:

Abide with me, fast falls the eventide:
The darkness deepens; Lord, with me abide:
When other helpers fail, and comforts flee,
Help of the helpless, O abide with me.

Swift to its close ebbs out life's little day;
Earth's joys grow dim, its glories pass away;
Change and decay in all around I see:
O thou who changest not, abide with me.

I need thy presence every passing hour;
What but thy grace can foil the tempter's power?
Who like thyself my guide and stay can be?
Through cloud and sunshine, Lord, abide with me.

I fear no foe with thee at hand to bless;
Ills have no weight, and tears no bitterness.
Where is death's sting? Where, grave, thy victory?
I triumph still, if thou abide with me.

Hold thou thy Cross before my closing eyes;
Shine through the gloom, and point me to the skies:
Heaven's morning breaks, and earth's vain shadows flee;
In life, in death, O Lord, abide with me.

2. Picture the Risen Lord standing before you. Seek to know
that you are in His Presence. Speak to Him by name. Say,
'Jesus', and in saying His name seek to express your love. Say it
again and again, to express your longing and love for Him.

Now picture someone who needs your prayers. See that He
is with them. Again say, 'Jesus'. Express your love for Him and
for them. Know that He is with them and offers His love. See
each of them surrounded and bathed in His light. Know that
in Him we triumph, and that we are all in Him. In time, move
to someone else who needs your prayer and meet Jesus there,
again call His name.

End this prayer with an affirmation of His love and His promise that in Him all will be well.

Christ is the morning star, Who when the night of this world is past, promises and reveals to His saints the eternal life of light.[13]

3. Make this prayer from the island of Benbecula your own.

O Being of life! O Being of peace!
O Being of time, and time without cease!
O Being, infinite, eternity!
O Being, infinite, eternity!

In good means of life be thou keeping me.
In all good intending, o keeping be,
Be keeping me always in good estate,
Far better than I know to supplicate,
    O better than I know to supplicate!

Be shepherding me for all this day long,
Relieve my distress, relieve me from wrong,
Enfold me this night with thine arms' embrace,
And pour upon me thy bountiful grace,
    O pour upon me thy bountiful grace!

My speaking and words do thou guard for me,
And strengthen for me my love, charity,
Illumine for me the stream I must o'er
And succour thou me when I pass death's door,
    O succour thou me when I pass death's door![14]

4. Learn that:

'He is risen'
That through Him we may discover faith:
in ourselves
in our world
in our God.

'He is risen'
That in Him we may rekindle hope:
for the abandoned
for the despairing
for the dreamless.

158

'He is risen'
That in Him we may restore love:
to those from whom we have kept it
to those who are most near to us
to those we will never meet
to all and everything.

'He is risen.'[15]

NOTES

INTRODUCTION

1 Gerald Murphy, *Early Irish Lyrics*, Oxford 1956.

BE THOU MY VISION

1 Minnie Louise Hoskins, 'God Knows'.
2 I Samuel 3.1–10.
3 Alexander Carmichael, ed. *Carmina Gadelica*, Academic Press, vol. i, p. 39.
4 Athanasian Creed, *Book of Common Prayer*.
5 John 9.25.
6 Teilhard de Chardin, *Hymn of the Universe*, Collins/ Fontana 1970, p. 79.
7 Teilhard de Chardin, *Le Milieu Divin*, Collins/Fontana 1964, p. 46.
8 Proverbs 20.18.
9 William Blake, 'A Memorable Fancy'.
10 John 20.11—21.24.
11 John 1.14.
12 G. R. D. McLean, *Poems of the Western Highlanders*, SPCK 1961, p. 261. Also in McLean, *Praying with Highland Christians*, SPCK/Triangle 1988, p. 30.
13 George Herbert, 'The Elixir'.
14 Alistair MacLean, *Hebridean Altars*, Edinburgh 1937, p. 101.

LORD OF MY HEART

1 Robert Louis Stevenson, 'Happy Thought'.
2 T. S. Eliot, 'Choruses from *The Rock*' from *Collected Poems 1909–1962*, Faber 1963.
3 See Matthew 12.43–5.
4 Psalm 84.2, *Book of Common Prayer*.
5 *Hebridean Altars*, p. 77.

6   *Poems of the Western Highlanders*, p. 8; *Praying with Highland Christians*, p. 5.

7   ibid., p. 90.

8   *Carmina Gadelica*, vol. iii, p. 25.

9   Peter Toon, *Meditating upon God's Word*, Darton, Longman and Todd 1988, p. 95.

10 *Carmina Gadelica*, vol. iii, p. 339.

11 *Hebridean Altars*, p. 129.

12 *Poems of the Western Highlanders*, p. 368.

13 *Hebridean Altars*, p. 55.

14 *Alternative Service Book 1980*, Order for Holy Communion, p. 119.

ALL ELSE BUT NAUGHT

1   Percy Bysshe Shelley, 'Ozymandias'.

2   T. S. Eliot, *East Coker*, V, from *Four Quartets*, Faber 1942.

3   Tacitus, *Agricola*, 30.

4   Deuteronomy 8.2–6, Jerusalem Bible.

5   Mark 1.12–13, Jerusalem Bible.

6   Isaiah 35.1–8, Good News Bible.

7   Bede, *A History of the English Church and People*, bk.iii, ch. 23 and bk.iv, ch. 28; trs. Leo Sherley-Price, Penguin 1955, pp. 177, 256.

8   R. Campbell, *Letters from a Stoic*, Penguin 1969, p. 75.

9   Quoted in Helen Waddell, *The Desert Fathers*, Constable p. 7.

10 Thomas Merton, *The Wisdom of the Desert*, Darley Andersen Books 1988, p. 22.

11 Hosea 2.14, GNB

12 G. D. R. McLean, 'Pilgrimage', *Poems of the Western Highlanders*, p. 55.

13 Psalm 42.1–2 *Book of Common Prayer*.

14 Maria Boulding, *The Coming of God*, SPCK 1982, p. 7.

THOU MY BEST THOUGHT

1   Kuno Meyer, *Selections from Ancient Irish Poetry*, Constable 1928, p. 35.

2   Arnold Marsh, tr., *St Patrick's Writings*; Confessions, Dundalk, Dunalgan, p. 53.

3   Ramon Lull, *The Book of the Lover and the Beloved*, sect.
    61; trs. Alison Peers, SPCK 1978.
4   John Denver, *Annie's Song*. Copyright © Cherry Lane
    Music Ltd., London.
5   From *Aspects of Love*, music: Andrew Lloyd Webber, lyric:
    Don Black and Charles Hart. Copyright © 1988 The
    Really Useful Group plc, London.
6   Mark 12.33.
7   *Thesaurus Palaeohibernicus*.
8   *Carmina Gadelica*, vol. iii, p. 145.
9   *Poems of the Western Highlanders*, p. 7. Also in *Praying
    With Highland Christians*, p. 3.
10 ibid.
11 ibid.
12 Kuno Meyer, *Ancient Irish Poetry*. See also David Adam,
    The Cry of the Deer, SPCK/Triangle 1987, p. 3.
13 George Appleton, *The Word is the Seed*, SPCK 1976, p. 49.

BE THOU MY WISDOM

1   *Poems of the Western Highlanders*, p. 361. Also *Praying
    With Highland Christians*, p. 78.
2   *Le Milieu Divin*, p. 112.
3   Genesis 28.16.
4   Psalm 33.4–6, *Book of Common Prayer*.
5   Psalm 29.3–4, *Book of Common Prayer*.
6   *Ancient Irish Poetry*, p. 100.
7   G. A. F. Knight *Psalms*, vol. 1 Daily Study Bible, Saint
    Andrews Press 1982, p. 141.
8   Proverbs 3.19.
9   Wisdom of Solomon, 9.2.
10 *Carmina Gadelica*, vol. i, p. 45.
11 ibid., vol. iii, p. 117.
12 1 John 4.20.
13 Quoted in Kallistos Ware, *The Orthodox Way*, Mowbray
    1979, p. 58.
14 Sydney Carter, 'Lord of the Dance'. Copyright © Stainer
    & Bell Ltd,.

THY PRESENCE MY LIGHT

1 Jonah, 1.3, 10.
2 Psalm 139.6–11, *Book of Common Prayer*.
3 Jacques Maritain, *Degrees of Knowledge*, Bles, Centenary Press, 1937.
4 Thomas Merton, *Seeds of Contemplation*, Anthony Clark, 1972, p. 230.
5 *Carmina Gadelica*, vol. iii, p. 145.
6 *Poems of the Western Highlanders*, p. 57, *Praying With Highland Christians*, p. 76.
7 ibid., p. 7.
8 ibid., p. 319.
9 ibid., p. 222.
10 Martin Reith, *God in our Midst*, SPCK/Triangle, 1975, 1989, p. 49.
11 Exodus 33.14.
12 Thomas Traherne, *Centuries*, Mowbray 1985, p. 14.
13 *Carmina Gadelica*, vol. iii, p. 53.

THOU MY GREAT FATHER

1 *Hebridean Altars*, p. 99.
2 Romans 8.22.
3 Psalm 24.1, *Book of Common Prayer*.
4 Alex King, *Wordsworth and the Artist's Vision*, 1966, p. 20.
5 Romans 8.28.
6 *Hymn of the Universe*, p. 25.
7 Exodus 33.17 KJV.
8 Isaiah 45.3 KJV.
9 Matthew 10.29–31 GNB.
10 John 1.10–13 KJV and GNB.
11 *Hebridean Altars*, p. 99.
12 ibid., p. 92.
13 Julian of Norwich, *A Shewing of God's Love*, ed. Anna Maria Reynolds, Sheed and Ward 1984.
14 E. Milner-White, *My God, My Glory*, SPCK 1959, p. 102.

THOU MY WHOLE ARMOUR

1 Psalm 23.1, 4 *Book of Common Prayer*.
2 Psalm 91.1–7 *Book of Common Prayer*.

3   *Early Irish Lyrics*, p. 35.
4   Romans 8.31.
5   2 Kings 6.8–16.
6   *Early Irish Lyrics*, p. 23.
7   Romans 8.38–9 GNB.
8   *A Shewing of God's Love.*
9   *Carmina Gadelica*, vol. iii, p. 105.
10 *Hebridean Altars*, p. 122.

GREAT POWER OF MY POWER

1   Isaiah 46.4 KJV.
2   John Henry Newman.
3   Charles Causley, 'I am the great sun', from a Normandy crucifix of 1632. *Collected Poems 1951–75*, Macmillan, 1975, p. 69.
4   John 10.10.
5   Gerard Manley Hopkins, 'The Wreck of the *Deutschland*'.
6   Luke 15.5–6 RSV.
7   Ephesians 4.9–10 KJV.
8   Oscar Wilde, *E Tenebris.*
9   *A Shewing of God's Love.*
10 Gerard Manley Hopkins, 'The Wreck of the *Deutschland*'.
11 Isaiah 43.1–2 KJV.
12 Exodus 33.14.
13 *Poems of the Western Highlanders*, p. 333; *Praying With Highland Christians*, p. 37.
14 ibid., p. 336; *Praying With Highland Christians*, p. 36.
15 Christina Rossetti. *Selected Poems*, Carcanet 1984, p. 64.
16 Collect for the Fourth Sunday after Epiphany, *Book of Common Prayer.*

MY TREASURE THOU ART

1   Matthew 14.45 GNB.
2   *Ancient Irish Poetry*, pp. 47–51.
3   *History of the English Church*, bk. iii, ch. 26.
4   A. E. Taylor, *Faith of a Moralist*, Macmillan 1937, p. 307.
5   Quoted in Waddell, *The Desert Fathers*, p. 30.
6   Thomas Traherne, *Centuries*, p. 6.

7   ibid., p. 7.
8   ibid., p. 14.
9   Dietrich Bonhoeffer, *The Cost of Discipleship*, SCM 1959, p. 36.
10 George Appleton, *The Word is the Seed*, p. 74.

THOU HEAVEN'S BRIGHT SUN

1   Luke 1.78–9.
2   Tom Stoppard, *Jumpers*, Faber 1986.
3   Gerard Manley Hopkins, *God's Grandeur*.
4   *Hymn of the Universe*, p. 35.
5   *Hebridean Altars*, p. 55.
6   ibid., p. 25.
7   Philippians 4.4–8 RSV.
8   John 16.33 RSV.
9   1 Corinthians 15.57–8 RSV.
10 William Walsham How, 'For all the saints'.
11 J. Patterson Smyth, *A People's Life of Christ*, Hodder and Stoughton, p. 25.
12 2 Corinthians 4.7–9 GNB.
13 The Venerable Bede.
14 *Poems of the Western Highlanders*, p. 81.
15 From a prayer card of the Additional Curates' Society.

Also published by
TriΛNGLE

THE EDGE OF GLORY:

Prayers in the Celtic tradition

by David Adam

A simplicity, a directness, a freshness, a spirituality is the essence of this book of prayers which can be for private, group or congregational use. They convey 'the abiding presence that never leaves us or forsakes us'.

Church News

Simple, yet deep, prayers which bring with them an atmosphere of the immanence of God, and do truly touch 'the edge of glory'.

Family Life Newsline

It is a style that beautifully combines God's glory with everyday events. Containing prayers for individual devotions and corporate worship, they all express joyful faith in God.

Christian Family

Apart from the prayers which are very evocative of a mood of peace and acceptance, rooted in the ordinary things of daily life, there are some beautiful line drawings and illustrations in the Celtic style.

Ely Review

THE CRY OF THE DEER

Meditations on the Hymn of St Patrick

by David Adam

Following the popularity of *The Edge of Glory*, David Adam continues to explore the Celtic way of prayer.

The Cry of the Deer takes us deeper into the prayer experience through a series of meditations leading into practical exercises in affirming the Presence of God through prayer. These meditations are based on the eternal certainties of the Christian faith, as acclaimed in the translation of the Hymn of St Patrick known as 'The Deer's Cry'. They are designed to help us to experience faith not merely as creeds but as a vital, living relationship with God which touches every aspect of our lives.

TIDES AND SEASONS

Modern prayers in the Celtic tradition

by David Adam

Once again David Adam draws from the rich store of Celtic spirituality insights which speak to our condition. The prayers he has written for this book echo the rhythms of creation which find their parallels in our spiritual lives. The movement of the tides – incoming, full flood, ebb tide, low tide – are linked to the cycle of the year, the seasons of life, and the highs and lows of our own experience. In the lives of each of us, many strong currents are at work. Yet in the ebb and flow nothing is lost, only changed. The sea of God's love is not diminished. Even in times of despair, we are made aware that there are other shores, eternal reaches, and after the lowest ebb the tide will flow again.

Praying with
HIGHLAND CHRISTIANS

G. R. D. McLean

Foreword by Sally Magnusson

A selection of prayers from G. R. D. McLean's translations of traditional Gaelic poems, *Poems of the Western Highlanders*. Though they arise out of a social structure now largely vanished, they deal with the unchanging basics of human life – with bodily needs, the daily round, family love, our fears and temptations and the need for security.

'A refreshing reminder of the great riches of our own heritage . . . Page after page vibrates with a 'glory' which for many has passed away from the earth.'

David Adam

'It is a privilege to pray with these Celtic Christians. Their conversations with the God they loved all those years ago must surely enhance our own, just as their humanity and their faith can only enlarge ours.'

Sally Magnusson